DADDY'S TURN

Terry Cummings, LCSW
760-285-5043
714-402-0279

DADDY'S TURN

*A Random Collection of Thoughts From the Green
and Docile Hill Called Fatherhood*

Ray Bransky

DADDY'S TURN
Ray Bransky

Printed by:
Quadco Printing
Chico, California

Printing History

First Edition—December, 1997

ISBN: 0-9661474-0-5

Editors: Jennifer Herron-Bransky, Laurie Clifton
Cover Photography: Chris Kaufman
Layout, cover design and illustrations: Rob Warner

As always,
to horses,
bunnies
and
loaders.

CONTENTS

Father's Day. 1

Trick or Treat?. 3

Dad's Night Out. 5

Ray's Wife is Pregnant 7

One Man's Riches. 10

Weekday Coffee 12

Michael's Wedding 14

Bill's Christmas 17

Whispering a Prayer 19

Keep the Tip. 20

Things I Forgot About Babies 23

Through the Eyes of a Two-Year-Old. 26

Bonding With My Son 28

My Wife's Story. 31

Seals Like Me. 34

Thanksgiving 36

Holiday Magic 38

My Sleeping Son 40

Living in the Past 42

First Overnight 44

No Time for Intimacies 47

Aunt Marilee 49

A Remembrance from Fall 52

The Candy Land Cognitive
  Development Skills
  Assessment Test. 55
Two Pictures 58
Daddy All Gone 60
Kite Day 62
Value in a Yard Sale 64
A Tale of Two Fathers 67
The Arcade 69
ABCs 71
Another Tuesday Night 73
Mike Grew Up. 75
Family Vacations 78
Southside. 81
Playdough 83
George's Father 86
Buying a Bike 89
Bears Don't Read 92
Lunch 95
A Delicate Matter 97
Graduation Overnight 100
Paper or Plastic 103
A Poem Found 106

FORWARD

I first started writing a column in April of 1992. It was published in a series of weekly newspapers in California's Central Valley, and, at the time, I wrote mostly about life in a small town community. As I grew as a father, I found that my writing tended to be more family oriented. So, I had an idea to write something specifically from a father's point of view. I shopped it around for a year or so, and eventually found a daily that would run it every other week.

Daddy's Turn was born.

I am thankful for the opportunity to have a column which is published. In all honesty though, there is a stronger incentive that keeps me at the keyboard week after week.

That would be my deadline.

Early on in my writing career, I discovered that there was no greater foe nor friend than that 11th hour siren that beckons me.

Life as a parent affords little time for luxuries. From the time we wake to when our exhausted personages lie prone at day's end, our lives are filled with all the little details of parenthood. From feedings and soccer games, to Boy Scout camp-outs and senior proms, there is never enough time to sit back, enjoy and reflect.

The idea of having a simple deadline, however, forces me to do just that. If I didn't have one, I fear that my life as a father could pass me by as I hectically scurry from one parental duty to the next.

And though it sometimes feels like a vulture circling over my shoulder, my deadline forces me to take some needed time off as a parent and consider the blessings I have.

What follows is an excerpt of a column I wrote in October of 1994. It explains why I do what I do with the 700 words I am allotted each week. More importantly, I hope it adequately illustrates how much I value my deadline and how much I appreciate you, as readers, for giving me one.

What I Leave Behind

The reason I write is because of a lamp. A lamp that sits in our living room atop a round table by the hall door. It is an old fixture and the living room that it sits in belongs to an old house. All modesty aside, the lamp looks very good in this room, in this house.

The antiqued finish of the base actually holds up two lamps that are each wrapped in white glass globes. A delicate floral pattern colors the white glass and shades any direct brightness. Twin hurricane chimneys peak the top.

For years, whenever my mother would visit she would unfailingly comment on how beautiful that lamp looked in our living room. She would sit in the chair across from it and smile as if it were an old friend. After a few moments, with a glimmer in her eye she would speak of the time when she had bought that lamp.

"It was the first job I ever had," she would start. "And it was with the first paycheck I ever earned... That lamp is older than your sister." she would always say. She would then tell us how she wanted to get just a little something for herself to celebrate her new found status of employment.

This story always led into another. Usually the one about how infuriated my father was that she made more money at the phone company than he did as an educator, and how he left teaching to become an aerospace engineer just so he could make more money than his wife.

Invariably, this would lead to a string of other stories that we heard each time she visited and admired this lamp.

When my mother passed away, she took most of those tales with her.

Some I remember. I remember the one about how scared she was when she was eight years old. She was sitting on the bed of her dying mother. I remember the story when she tried to poison her brother by putting iodine in his orange juice. And yes, I remember the one about our lamp. I'm fortunate that I will be able to recount these narratives to my children, but there are countless others that my son and daughter will never hear.

We will never know about the duck my mother had as a child, and I know the names of the dogs that protected her in the woods of Connecticut are gone forever. What about all those concoctions her grandmother used to relieve fevers and illness? Where was the homestead cabin her grandmother was born in? In which state park is it located? Which grandmother was it who thought she had a tumor when she delivered her twelfth child on the dining room table? Or was it her thirteenth?

All gone.

I guess there are really two reasons why I write, for myself and for my children. I write so that when I am old and my memory pales, I will be able to remember. I will remember the smell of new cut grass and the warmth of a newborn's breath. I will remember how I fell in love with that girl in pig tails and blue jeans.

I also write so that if anything happens to me, my children will know who I am. They will know that I laughed. They will know that I lived through joyous and difficult times. They will know how much it meant to hold their hands and to watch them dream. They will know that I loved them. And I write so my children and grandchildren will know how beautiful a lamp looks in their living room.

What follows is a collection of columns that I have written. There is no underlying theme as they are simply laid out chronologically in the order they were written. There is no deeper meanings, no grand design. Some are stories about my family. Some may be of yours. I think you'll find, however, they all tell the many tales of fatherhood.

ACKNOWLEDGEMENTS

To think that any task is accomplished through one's own efforts is to deny oneself the true satisfaction of a job well done.

It is in this spirit that I would like to thank everyone who has provided me the support and encouragement each week when I sit down to tell my story.

First, I would like to thank my children for the visions they gladly share with me and the undying source of inspiration they unselfishly provide. Next would be my wife. If there is anyone to whom the credit for Daddy's Turn should really go, it would be her, my loving companion, the mother of my children, and the stout hearted junior high English teacher who dutifully stands my side with a trusty red pen in hand as I burn the midnight oil. Without her wisdom, direction and constructive guidance, I would never have even known where to start.

I would also like to thank Laurie Clifton, my editor at the Chico Enterprise-Record who patiently corrects all of the mistakes that I thought my wife was wrong about. Thanks also needs to be given to Jack Winning for giving me the opportunity to share my "voice" and the tales it tells. The cover photo was taken by Chris Kaufman, whose wonderful talents confidently captured the essence of fatherhood. Not bad for a green horn photo-journalist fresh out of college.

I also need to acknowledge Rob Warner for the great job he did in the book layout, cover design and illustrations. When I asked if he had children, he said "No, but I have animals. Does that help?" Apparently it does.

A special thank you goes out to all of my friends who, intentionally or not, were a valuable source for material when my creative inkwell ran dry. I would also like to recognize everyone at Parent Education Network for their undying encouragement and enthusiasm.

Lastly, I would like to thank my parents, Howard and Jean, for giving me the tools I need for the most important job I will ever have. Fatherhood.

FATHER'S DAY

I don't know how many times this has happened to me.

I was napping in the Lazy Boy, with the windows to my left wide open. The sounds of spring filled my ears as a warm breeze bathed me.

A noise startled me from my sleep, and for just a flash, there I was, 20-some-odd years ago, playing soccer at Mildred Morrow Elementary School. My back was all itchy from the bermuda and the smell of fresh cut grass filled my head. It was all so real.

Then, in another flash, I was back in my chair with a faint smile on my lips and that spring breeze bringing in the perfume of my neighbor's mowing.

It happens like that. Some sound or smell will stir memories in me I would never be able to consciously bring back. Wonderful times in my life that could remain forever lost.

A few months ago we spent the weekend with my folks. They have a rather small home now. There's just a couple of bedrooms, a laundry room and a kitchen that opens to a living area. I bring this up only to illustrate how crowded it can be when the whole family visits. Which is usually what happens.

I live about seven hours south of my parents and my brother and sister live about six hours to the north. Because none of us want to drive thirteen hours to see each other, we always decide to meet at the folks.

My sister and her family sleep in the converted attic over the garage.

My brother and his dog stay in the R.V. in the driveway. My parents naturally sleep in their room, and because we have the youngest child, we stay in the bedroom upstairs from them.

My brother is always the first one up and starts his day with an hour long walk with his dog. When I can pry myself out of bed, I like being the next up. It gives me a little sanity time before the whole house is filled. My father used to get up at the crack of dawn, but retirement has forced him to enjoy sleeping in.

My daughter has always been a good sleeper. She always wakes up happy and excited for the new day.

I had just finished my first cup of coffee when I heard her rattle the crib. The slightest whisper can be heard throughout the house, so I tried to reach upstairs before she shook everyone awake. When I peeked in with my finger to my lips, she lit up with a great smile and screamed, "Daddy!" with unquenchable joy.

I picked her up and swept her to the bathroom to get her changed and dressed. When we came downstairs, Grandpa sat at the table. His hair was all scrunched to the side and wrinkles were still on his face from sleeping. I apologized for waking him, but he just shrugged it off. As he took his granddaughter onto his lap, he said it was wonderful to wake up to the sound of a happy child.

A few minutes later, I looked over the egg pan to see the two of them reading, and I couldn't help but wonder...

Before we came downstairs, was there a flash when my father awoke some 30 years back, rolled over with a faint smile, and breathed the words, "Good morning Ray Ray."

May, 1992

TRICK OR TREAT?

Halloween was over one week ago, but it was only just recently we were able to look back and laugh. This was to be our daughter's first real Halloween. The first time she would dress up, go to the carnivals and trick or treat.

I was to research the activities and plan our ghoulish agenda. My wife's task was to assemble the costume, and it was the sole responsibility of my daughter to be happy and healthy at the appointed haunting hour. No easy task for a 2-year-old.

Mid-October my wife and I began thumbing through the latest issue of Parents Magazine. It was the one with all the costume ideas that could be created in less than one hour. In fact, they didn't even have to be sewn. They could be glued. The choice was easy. It had to be the tiger. She loved her stuffed tiger. The only thing she held in higher esteem was Big Bird, but you just can't make a Big Bird in less than an hour, with or without glue.

So it was decided. Our princess was to be a tiger.

The next weekend, materials were purchased. Two days later, construction had begun, and by Halloween morning, my wife pretty much had that tiger by the tail. The project did take longer than the promised "a little less than an hour." However, since the first event wasn't until late afternoon, the costume was finished with plenty of time to spare. Perhaps 15 minutes, maybe even 20. It was hard for me to tell. I was busy trying to stay out of my wife's way. Hell hath no fury like that of a woman scorned by a Halloween costume.

When it was completed, the car was pretty much packed and snacks were in the cooler. So, all we had to do was get our daughter into the costume, and we could head down the road.

Within moments we realized a grievous error had been committed. An error so large and so heinous it threatened our existence as parents.

We had left out the input of one tiny, little individual 2-year-old.

"It's time to put on your costume, Honey."

"No."

"Don't you want to trick or treat?"

"Yes."

"Then you have to have a costume to go trick or treat," and we slowly slipped the orange and black poncho over her head.

"No!" was the word that echoed through our happy home as she unglued most of the outfit while she ripped every last bit of fake tiger fur from around her neck. We tried for half an hour to get her into that outfit, but no amount of encouragement, persuasion or bribery could convert our little angel into a tiger.

I looked deep into my wife's eyes. Eyes that were brimming with tears of a woman who had failed in her most basic of maternal duties. I held her hand and said, "I think her overalls are clean. Maybe she'd like to be a farmer."

That day I learned Halloween was a holiday to be celebrated by children. A holiday where they can pretend to be whatever they want to be, limited by their imaginations only. Our job was to put in long, frustrating, thankless hours to ensure they become the tiger they want to be.

Last August, while we were visiting my wife's relatives, her aunt passed on a bit of wisdom to us. It is knowledge I hope to pass on to my children someday.

My wife was seated in front of their antique pump organ with her feet going at a furious pace on the pedals. Our daughter was on her lap playing the sweet and peaceful melodies of youth. My wife stopped for a moment to catch her breath, and as she started anew, her aunt patted her shoulder and said, "That's your duty now in life. You pump while your children play."

November, 1992

4

Dad's Night Out

As you know, I'm a relatively new father. My daughter is almost 20 months of age. For the first 10 months or so, my wife attended a post-postpartum support group. They called it a Mom's Group.

She claims these weekly meetings were of great benefit because of the sharing that went on between new mothers. You know. What works for colic. How to get baby to sleep without a bottle. That sort of stuff. She says if nothing else, it's good to see others having the same problems as us. We're not alone.

Just between you and I, I think what they really talk about is how their husbands have the gall to have breasts that won't lactate and how we haven't changed a poopy in weeks.

Well, the first one is out of my hands, so to speak. I try my best, but this cow is dry. Now for the latter. I can't help it if our darling's bathroom habits take after mine. She's like clock work. At 10 o'clock, after breakfast and a stimulating cup of juice, she picks up a copy of Good Morning Chick and heads off to start her day. By that time I'm already at work, with a hot cup of coffee and the latest issue of People Magazine.

So, where is all of this leading?

A group of us fathers decided we should get together and share ideas. Boy, there is nothing better than sitting around with a bunch of guys on a Friday night, a beer in one hand, a fist full of pork rinds in the other, swapping valiant tales of diaper rash and projectile vomiting.

Now, that's bonding.

There's a tricky part though. Out of these Dad's Nights comes some really great stories. The question is, as I relay them to you, should I tell them from the point of view of the original father, or take some creative liberty and steal them for myself? I don't believe there is an easy answer.

Let me give you an example.

At one of these get-togethers, a father shared this with us. One day last summer, when he was working without a shirt, he took a break and picked up his daughter. Without hesitation, the infant latched on to his nipple and attempted to nurse. Because of this, he felt a little embarrassed. End of story.

This is how I would like to tell it.

After working for hours in the blazing sun, my wife emerged from the air-conditioned comfort of our domicile with my Princess on her hip. She handed her to me and walked back inside, mumbling something about my turn for the poopy. My daughter, not one to pass up an opportunity, immediately hoovered herself to my right nipple and sucked like there was no tomorrow.

It wasn't until 11 minutes later I was able to take a crowbar-like utensil from the garden shed and pry her precious little lips from the grapefruit sized blood blister that had formed.

The shame was unrelenting, the guilt, unbearable. My daughter tried to breast-feed on me! It was against nature. Maybe, against the law. It was . . . wrong.

Who knows the extent of the psychological damage done. I had scarred her for life. Twenty years from now, I can see myself saying it was all my fault. It was because of that one day so long ago that my precious pumpkin became an axe wielding serial killer! How could I live with myself?

I think you get the picture.

Oh well, there are no easy answers to such ethical dilemmas. Besides, it's time for me to go. My daughter's letting me know that she has a poopy with my name on it.

I wonder if she's been fed?

June, 1993

RAY'S WIFE IS PREGNANT!

I have exciting news!

If this were "Wheel of Fortune", Vanna would be spelling out "R Y'S W F S PR GN NT!". Here, let me help. I'll spring for the vowels.

Pat, I'd like to buy an A, an I and an E. "RAY'S WIFE IS PREGNANT!"

This is truly exciting news for a couple of reasons. Years ago, I got the word from my doctor that there would be a slim chance of me becoming a father. "Ray," he explained in a voice that was extremely sensitive to my delicate male ego, "the average man has about ten million of these little guys. You've only got one. Not one million. Just one."

I guess I must have found myself a regular Fertile Myrtle, because my wife and I are now doubly blessed.

The road to parenthood hasn't always been a smooth one, however. I've often found that the people who are to help you through these difficult times have the kindness and sensitivity of a door mat.

Every time, and I mean EVERY time, I was to leave a sample at the lab, the lab technicians gladly took the plastic jar, held it up to the light, shook it twice and said, "Are you sure you got all of it in there?"

"Yes," I'd answer with head held high.

"You didn't spill any?"

"Look, I was right there. I didn't spill any. I guess I'm just not the virile young stud you thought I was."

Really, what did they think I was there for? Did they think I thrived on this personal abuse of my masculinity.

I swear the labs only hire people who get turned down by the Department of Motor Vehicles.

Personnel Director: "Have you ever applied to the DMV?"
Applicant: "Yes."
Personnel Director: "Were you hired?"
Applicant: "No."
Personnel Director: "Can you start today?"

The doctors aren't always better. One urologist had me leave a urine sample with every office visit. When I had to leave the other, he could not refrain himself. He asked if I had gotten it all in there.

"Did you spill any?"

"Doc, for four weeks I've filled the urine cup to the brim. If I could, don't you think I would?"

And then, I'm forced to write him a check and say thank you. Honest, I'm not a masochist at heart.

Enough of my whining.

When we found out we were "with child", the first time, we used one of the home pregnancy tests. You know, the ones on TV where the woman looks deep into the man's eyes and says, "You're going to be a father."

We mixed the solution in vial one, put in couple drops of urine (hers not mine), dipped the little stick thingy in the vial for about thirty seconds and then let it set in vial two for ten minutes. If the stick was white, we'd try again next time. If it was blue, I got to go shopping for cigars.

We didn't want the waiting to be torturous, so we decided to play a game of foosball while the time passed. She was ahead six to four when the timer went off, but I was the first in the hall. We raced to the bathroom and being the first one there, I slammed the door shut and locked it.

Events like these, I believe, should be accompanied by a certain amount of pomp and ceremony. From the hollering, pounding, and threats coming from the other side of the door, I'd say my wife didn't agree.

I unlocked the door.

We both took a peek at the vial and patted ourselves on the back for a job well done.

June, 1993

ONE MAN'S RICHES

L ast Monday was a big day for us. As you know, my wife teaches, and last Monday was her first day back at school. It was also when my daughter was to be back at daycare. The week before, we took her back to the center for a little while just to get her used to it again, but Monday was to be her first full day back.

Fate, however, had other plans. At 5:30 A.M. we woke to find our little angel's head had filled with mucous and her breathing sounded like gravel being poured into a bucket. My wife and I drew straws to see who would be the one to stay home with her.

I'm still not sure if I won or lost.

Actually, there wasn't much of a choice. There is an unwritten rule that after three months off, a teacher doesn't miss the first day of school unless she's dead. Even then a note from the holy spirit is required. So, I was to stay home.

After a quick call to my boss, my daughter and I ate breakfast, got dressed and headed to the doctor's office. She was in pretty good spirits all things considered. She didn't complain a whole lot, and only once blew snot down the front of her sweater. It could have been worse.

We watched the fish in the waiting area until the nurse called us into the exam room.

The doctor came in a few minutes later. He listened here and looked there, wrote a couple of prescriptions and waved a magic lollipop to make everything better. He said if she improved by this evening, it would be okay to take her to daycare tomorrow.

As we walked to the pharmacy, I asked my daughter what she did with the doctor. She showed me how he looked into her ears and mouth and listened to her chest. When we arrived, we took a seat and started a game of "I see" to pass the time.

This is a game where I say that I see something, and she has to find it and say it too. This can be challenging with a two year old in a pharmacy.

"I see a laxative."

" LAXATIVE !"

I noticed an older gentleman that was seated next to us. He watched the game as intently as my daughter. They called his name and he stood up. At the last minute he turned to me with the kindest eyes and said, "She's your riches. No matter how much money, you'll never be richer than you are right now." He picked up his prescription, waved good bye and walked out of our lives.

At that point it was obvious that I had drawn the short straw and won. Isn't it odd, that it took me all day to figure out something that a perfect stranger saw right off.

August, 1993

Weekday Coffee

It is the last week of summer. Not the last of summer vacation, but the last of the season itself. The weather is turning. A cool breeze whispers through the trees most of the day. The calmness of fall is calling to me from just around the corner.

My daughter's birthday is coming in mid-October. She'll be two. Time, like the seasons, is passing, leaving me with not only memories of the past, but little peeks into the future. Perhaps a taste of things to come.

I was the one lucky enough to draw the short straw back at the office. I got to play hooky and go run for coffee. Fresh ground vanilla nut is what we all agreed on. So here I sit on a weekday at 10 o'clock. A time normally spent devoted to my clients and the telephone.

I sit in a coffee shop waiting for my order to be filled. I've been in this shop at least a dozen times before, but today it is a stranger. It is filled with unfamiliar sights and sounds.

It makes me sad.

The person behind the counter tells me the coffee once flavored, needs to set for a bit before it can be ground. Ten minutes or so and I can be on my way. I sit at a small table near the front. It has a wonderful view out the window to watch and wait while coffee is being flavored.

My attention wanders back inside though, to a group two tables down by the front door. It is a group of four adults and two children, all women, both girls. They were dressed in the comforts of sweat pants and baggy tee shirts. They spoke softly, and between whispers they sipped coffee and hot chocolate and nibbled on pastries. Another woman approached and set a cup down. As she sat, one of the girls said something I couldn't hear.

"Goodness!" she replied, "You've had two already?"

Then they went on talking in hushed melodies whose meanings escaped my ears.

On this weekday morning, I witness the communion of womankind as they whisper the wisdom and secrets of their gender from one generation to another, indeed, as they were passed to them from the beginning of all seasons. They tell not so much in words but in the actions and the feeling of the moment. Perhaps there is no agenda for these hidden truths to be shared. Perhaps they are only seeds of knowledge planted and nurtured, so they can grow and ripen into glorious discoveries ready for harvest.

It makes me wonder if this is something that will happen with my daughter and her mother. If a time will come where a part of my daughter will be hidden from me. Something only a mother will be able to enjoy. And as I ask myself this, I know deep inside what the answer will be.

And I turn away.

September, 1993

Michael's Wedding

"Eighteen years ago last month..." That's how I started my toast. My best friend, Michael, was married last week, and I was his best man. I had the opportunity to give the toast.

"I ask everyone to raise their glasses in toast. To Mike and Dawn, may you have a strong love and a long and happy marriage." Then we all drank to happiness and best wishes. At that point my official involvement in their day of nuptials was over.

To be honest, I wasn't as involved as I could have been. Sure I worked over eighteen years as his friend, but for the actual wedding preparations, I spent my time three hours away. I gave them my opinions when they were asked for. I bought the clothes they wanted me to wear, and I wrote my toast. I didn't become an active participant until their shower two weeks before.

We drove up north that Saturday afternoon and arrived at about five o'clock. The party started at five thirty, so we quickly cleaned up, dressed, and drove over to the home of the sister of the bride.

Even though Mike and I have been friends for so long, our lives are clearly different. This was evident by the folks my wife and I met. The backyard was packed with people, but the only ones we knew were Mike, his fiancee and his mother. Everyone though, did want to make us feel right at home.

Three women introduced themselves right away, and with the same breath, acknowledged my wife's condition.

"How far along are you?"

"Is it a boy or a girl?"

"Is that the varicose vein Dawn told us about?"

"Mine was bigger than that."

"Mine looked like a pineapple had grown out of the back of my knee."

A varicose vein had cropped up early on with the pregnancy, and it hasn't always been kind to my wife. We mentioned it only once to Mike and Dawn. When we RSVP'd we explained that we weren't sure if three hours in the car would aggravate it.

Good news apparently does travel fast. Within minutes of our arrival, my wife was surrounded by a frenzied hoard of postnatal mothers, all brandishing the battle scars of gestations past and showing the proper reverence to these badges of honor.

I went and got a beer.

After fifteen or twenty minutes, an eerie hush fell over the once frothing crowd. The matriarch was seated on a folding plastic chair. This throne was located at the heart of this pack. She leaned to one side and as she was about to speak, she lifted one leg. It was Michael's mother.

"See this?" she asked as a cigarette dangled from her lips. She raised her pant leg and pointed to the nastiest scar to be shown that night. All eyes followed her command and beheld the blessed blemish upon her ankle.

"I have another one just like it near my groin. Thirty-some years ago after I delivered my Michael, I had this one stripped. They clipped it at both spots and then ripped it clean through the whole length of the leg. It hurt a hundred times worse than the delivery, and I couldn't walk for almost a month the pain was so bad."

She glanced at her son with a look that showed how she would suffer the worst of all agony for her baby.

"See what you did to me?"

I went and got a beer for Mike.

That's pretty much how it went for the rest of the party and the wedding weekend. Most everyone focused on flowers, dresses and pregnancies.

When it was my turn to show my affections, I simply raised my glass and gave them a noble toast.

Hindsight is always so much clearer, and looking back, I think what I should have done was to pull Michael's pants down and point out where he he had been circumcised. Then he could look to his mother and say, "See what you did to me?"

I really think Mike would have liked that. I mean after eighteen years I should know.

October, 1993

Bill's Christmas

"I had been out of town for 10 days. My flight arrived on Christmas Eve, and we hadn't gotten a tree yet." Bill was telling me of a holiday past. "All the lots were sold out, so I stopped at the golf course and cut one down."

It had been many years since that particular yule tide celebration, but it was still fresh in his mind. It was one of the first Christmases he spent as a single parent almost 17 years ago.

It was the start of many beginnings for him and his family. He had sold the ski shop and was working for a large corporation. It was time he had gotten his life into perspective. He had sole custody of his two children, but it wasn't by choice. Bill's wife had passed away and left him a widower with a 3-year-old daughter and another that was less than 12 months.

When the rules are changed, how do you find the boundaries? How long would it take until you could look back and laugh at the possibility of failing your children on Christmas Eve? How does one face the daunting task of bringing two lives to maturity while leaving such an important part behind?

"I thought I handled it well, but looking back, I can see that I was pretty spaced." He told me the first year was pretty much a blur. He immersed himself in his business and did what he could for his kids.

"I had almost a million dollars of insurance on myself. There was nothing on her. It just wasn't something we thought of." He was the bread winner. Her services had to be paid out of savings.

In many ways he was a pioneer, breaking new ground for an evolving society. As a widower, his generation was perhaps a lost one. Those before him could have married again for convenience. Those following were understood as single parents. "I must have gone through 20 housekeepers that first year." Daycare was the exception, not the rule.

I had commented on how difficult it must have been, not just for him but for his daughters, to lose someone so close so suddenly. "In comparison," he said, "I think it was much easier than dragging them through months of divorce and custody battles." Which happens to many single parents. "It made me a better father. Before, I came home from work, bounced the girls on my knee and sent them to bed. After, I was forced to change diapers and get down and play with them."

I hope that time can heal all wounds. Sometimes I wake up in the middle of the night and slip from the bonds of warmth beside me, to make sure my daughter is all right. I'll press my hand to her cheek and ask that she not grow up too quickly. I'll then climb back into bed and let the cradle of my wife's breathing gently rock me back to sleep.

This is the essence of my life now, and to change this would be worse than asking me to forfeit my own soul.

In the end, it wasn't the chains of Jacob Marley's soul or the ghost of Christmas past that lead Bill to the golf course so many years ago. It was the spirit of a young man trying to do the best he could with the tools he had, the love for his children and his obligations to their mother.

December, 1993

Whispering a Prayer

His fingers were long and thin. The skin was bluish-grey and hung loose from the bones. The nails on each finger, were unusually long, as if they were unkept. His hands alternately fell open and then clamped shut, tight enough to whiten the knuckles.

When I first saw him, he was in the center of the room, gasping for air. Each breath rattled his lungs until he cried out for his thirst to be quenched. A breath that could clear his senses. A breath that could reassure him of his footing in this life. A breath that would come.

I was asked to hold him and comfort him. And in as much, I was asked to give him warmth, and to commit to him that I would protect him from the evils in his world.

I was asked to love him.

His head and body were stained with the blood of his ordeal. His eyes were black like the dust of coal and shined with the dullness of wonder.

I looked deep into those eyes, eyes that were wise beyond their years and drew him near. I told him it would be all right. I breathed a kiss of hope and held him to my breast.

Hours later, long after I had laid him to sleep, I walked out into the night and whispered a prayer. With each breath, I watched my request float into the cold December night and rise to the heavens in the hopes of being answered.

It was on this night that I met my son. A healthy boy, born to me with blind faith and unending love. And I pray that I may be worthy of him.

December, 1993

Keep the Tip

Have you ever noticed there's a difference between boys and girls?

I'm not talking about developmental, intellectual, or emotional differences. Nor am I talking about differences in societal or genetic influences. You know what I mean. How males are supposed to be genetically predisposed to be the warriors of civilization and the females are to be its nurturers.

I'm talking about the obvious contrast. The equipment that little boys have that enables them to shoot flies off the ceiling during the split-second that the dirty diaper is off but before the clean one is on. Little girls don't do that.

As a new parent of a 3-week-old boy, I find I am faced with a whole new set of dilemmas I didn't have with my daughter. Bragging rights, of course, are always a concern. I wasn't kidding about him shooting flies off the ceiling. If he can keep his distance proportionate with his body weight, he'll make a heck of a fireman someday. In all fairness though, he does need a little work on his accuracy.

Perhaps a more difficult quandary was the decision of whether to circumcise or not. Certainly a question we didn't have to think about with our little girl, and it wasn't an easy one this time around.

Should we, or shouldn't we? There is no longer any validity in the hygiene argument. Is social or religious conformity important enough to put his little nose to the grindstone so to speak?

We were so confident he wasn't going to be a boy, we didn't even settle on a name until the day we brought him home. I mean, after a sleepless night and 12 hours of labor, we just weren't ready to tackle this one.

So, we did what any other couple of the '90s would have done. We put it off. We set an appointment for day three of our young son's life. That would surely give us enough time to read up on circumcision, and confer with the proper authorities, our parents and our friends.

"We had it done to both of my boys," said my wife's colleague. "With my first son, I felt that if he was to be the one that had to go through with it, I should at least be there with him." He then told me how he valiantly stood outside the window of the room where the procedure was done. "In those days, I couldn't be in with him."

He explained they had his son in the type of gown where the sleeves fold over the hands. Their purpose is to keep the baby from scratching its eyes and delicate skin with its fingernails. On his son, however, one sleeve wasn't folded all the way over. There was room for a finger or two to find its way out. The young man was pretty quiet until the cut was made. When the steel met the flesh, this brave little soldier screamed out and thrust his one arm into the air, and out of that tiny little hole at the end of his sleeve popped up his middle finger.

How appropriate, I thought. The first act of defiance of a desperate man.

With that solid reassurance, I called my mother and asked her what had swayed her. She told me in those days, everyone did it. They didn't feel there was any real need for a choice to be made.

So, one week after my brother was born, she held her head high, handed him to the doctor and patiently waited. When it was over, the doctor emerged from the room with a bottle of elixir of terpin hydrate and two dosage cups. She told me that terpin hydrate was a cough syrup commonly known as "G.I. Gin" because of its high alcohol content. At this point I braced myself to hear how modern medicine of the 1950s prescribed 60 proof cough syrup for a week-old-infant.

"He poured a shot for me," my mother told me. "And when that was done, he poured one for himself."

We ended up doing a little more research and talked to a few more friends. In the end a decision was made, and it was one that my son, my wife and I will all have to live with.

He is sitting next to me at this moment, in his little chair, with his tiny blanket covering his lap. His eyes are closed, and he is enjoying the peaceful, innocent slumber of infancy. Another glance down tells me that if the rest of this story is to be told, it will have to wait. You see, it's not really mine to tell, but his.

January, 1994

Things I forgot About Babies

It happened when my wife was picking our daughter up at day-care. That's when she ran across a colleague of hers who had recently given birth to a little girl. She was picking up her two-year-old boy. Her baby was a little over one week of age. Our new son was six weeks and one day.

My wife asked if the baby was sleeping well at night. A tense smile was caught on her friend's face. A smile that spoke more than words ever could.

For the first few nights, our bouncing baby boy called for the breast quite often. It was every six and one half minutes that he would light into a sweet and soothing song for food. A song he embraced full of breath and strong of heart. It reminded me of the spring-like melodies that convicted murderers ring out on prison bars with tin cups.

Our son proved to be faithful to his emotions, for it was most of the darkened hours that he called to us with a voice so gentle, every six and one half minutes. It was on the third night that I asked myself if I would ever be paroled early for good behavior or whether I was facing a life sentence.

My wife shared a bit of this with her friend. Just enough to show she understood, but not so much as to put the fear of God into her. It was too late for them both. The axe had fallen and all our necks were on the chopping block. There was no need to make it worse. Why not make the best of the circumstances?

So, there they stood sharing tales of life with newborns and their two-year-old siblings. The stories told were not spoken with words or subtle glimmerings in their eyes, but rather, they were embedded in the dark circles that lay underneath them. Like petroglyphs carved into stone thousands of years ago, these stories lay bare for the world and all its generations to see.

I'm not telling this story to show how surprised I was at the amount of work involved with two children. Long before my wife and I decided to embark on Bountiful Harvest II, I had been reminded by everybody and their brother, who's had more than one child, just how much more difficult life would become when we were divinely blessed with yet another angel from heaven.

Nor am I complaining. There are moments, when I feel heavenly myself just holding my son and looking into his eyes.

What I am trying to illustrate is how surprised I have been at how much I've forgotten since the first one was born.

I'd forgotten how loud new babies cry. I'd forgotten how often they eat. I'd forgotten how much they poop, and I had certainly forgotten how little they sleep at night and how soundly they sleep during the day.

I'd forgotten how they hold a little of their poopy in until the diaper is off and then let'er loose on the towel. I'd also forgotten that they held in just a little more until the new diaper was on, and tore loose once again.

I had forgotten that babies always spit up on their clothes when we're headed out to the car, so we have to trudge everyone back in for a twenty minute wrestling match/outfit change. In fact, I had forgotten how long it took us to get ready to go anywhere. We have been invited over for dinner at some friends' house next Sunday. We started getting ready last Thursday, and we'll still probably be a day or two late.

I'd forgotten that shower gifts need to be used immediately or else the three month sleeper will be too small at one month.

I didn't forget how wobbly their heads are, but I had forgotten how sore my back got trying to cradle them against my shoulder. Quasimodo would have been a natural for those late night laps around the dining room table, holding with one arm and patting a back with the other.

I'd forgotten that the distance a newborn vomits is in direct proportion with the length of the parent's arms. I forgot how much of my wardrobe is dry clean only.

I had forgotten that my daughter had done all of those things a little over two years ago.

We've kept a diary for my daughter to mark and document all the milestones she has passed since birth. The first time she rolled over. The first time she drank formula and her first solid foods. The first time she slept in her own room and not ours. The first time she screamed S#@t at the top of her lungs.

When my son was five-weeks-old and barely sleeping an hour straight through, we looked in this diary to see what my daughter was doing at that age. Over two years ago my wife had written that at six weeks, she was sleeping through the night with only one feeding. Like ice cubes in the underworld, my wife and I knew there was no chance of that happening this time around. Yet, one week later, our little man was sleeping through with only two feedings and working on cutting back on those.

Nature has a funny way of helping us through times of trouble by allowing us to forget bygone occasions that were less than positive. When looking through the diaries of our daughter and our seven-week-old son, I now wonder if it would have been more appropriate to write about the things I haven't forgotten about babies.

I haven't forgotten the warmth and sweetness of their breath. I haven't forgotten the radiance of their first smile. And I haven't forgotten that when I hold their quiet and trusting bodies in my arms, I can think of nothing else but the love I have for them. A love that will last much longer than a sleepless night.

January, 1994

Through the Eyes of a Two-Year-Old

The wind rushes down the hillside, blows through my hair and sends me soaring above the treetops. Indeed, it is not everyday I find myself in the pasture, with my daughter in my lap, and a string of a kite clenched tightly in our hands.

I am truly blessed to have a little Messiah next to me whose touch can heal my blinded eyes, so I can see the world around me as it should be. Viewed through the eyes of a 2-year-old.

With my legs on the ground and my daughter next to me, I can fly high above to touch the hawks and eagles around me. Indeed, a cotton string is the only thing that anchors me to the earth. It is also the umbilical that pulls me toward the heavens.

When I turn, I can see my daughter crossing the pasture. As she walks through a patch of broadleaf weeds, it transforms into a dense jungle filled with panthers, hyenas and brightly colored birds. Danger is just a machete cut away.

This isn't something that happens all the time. Unfortunately, it's not even something I can reproduce at will. The sights, sounds, and smells have to be just right, and my daughter can just giggle or give my hand a squeeze, and I'm right there. I'm seeing life as she sees it.

The first time I rode with her on the back of our old mare, my daughter was sitting in front of me. She grabbed a handful of mane and through a tight lipped, mile-wide smile she said, "Daddy, I riding Lady." That was all it took. Our little acre and a half was now the untamed west. The green pasture had become the valley with the high chaparral up on the hill. The hanging tree was down by the barn.

Earlier in the year I was invited into her playhouse. The weather was a little nippy, but as we sat by the table, drinking pretend cups of hot cocoa, we found ourselves in a log cabin. The fire was keeping us warm. A good thing, too. The snow wasn't going to let up until the drifts reached the bottom of the windows.

On more than one occasion the play set with its slide and ladders has become a fort or a ship with flags hoisted high. The horses' water trough has been an ocean where giant goldfish plow the depths, while we sailed the surface in schooners of leaves. The braided rug in the living room has been the fertile ground that Tonkas till.

I often find myself more enraptured in my daughter's world than she is. When my plane has landed or the sailboat has docked, I'll find that my daughter has hung up the robes of a Messiah, and with those tasks completed, she has gone on to greater explorations.

I see another kite rise into the air three fields away. A chorus of cheers heralds its ascent. I smile to myself, happy to know, that perhaps, another Savior has helped another lost soul. Helped them to see through the eyes of a 2-year-old.

April, 1994

Bonding With My Son

Our home is located on a highway that is rather busy with traffic. I am sitting on a padded sweater chest. The kind that holds family valuables and memories and whose insides smell like a clean hamster cage on Saturday morning. My son is seated on my lap.

The three of us, my son, myself and the sweater chest are in front of the dining room window which faces the front lawn. At the edge of the lawn we can see the low fence with a gate at the walk. Beyond it are a few weeds that need mowing and adjacent to that is the asphalt trail which leads to the timberline and the coast.

We sit and watch images flash past and then patiently wait for more to appear. It is my job to call each out as it makes its presentation.

"Truck, truck, truck ... car."

My daughter took a bottle from me at an early age. This gave my wife the chance to take a night or two off each week. Time for herself, to work out or to have a night away with a friend. More importantly, it gave me a chance to spend some personal time with my daughter, eye to eye and belly to belly.

Mothers often say the most intense time they spent with their children was when they were breast feeding. They say it was the bonding that made it such a strong and personal experience.

"Car, car, truck-boat, car."

I can only speak from my Evenflo evenings, but I do feel that a special bond was established with my daughter and myself. It was a time we had to ourselves that allowed us to meet each other on our own terms. A time when we learned she could depend on me, and I on her.

Those were special times.

"Truck, van ... car, car, truck."

My son has not been so successful with a bottle. In almost all cases, he has provided my wife and I a whole host of challenges we didn't have with our daughter. The bottle issue, however, has been the most tenacious.

It's not just with me. Whether at the hands of his mother, grandmother, grandfather, or whoever, bottles are a caution to my son. In fact, after five months, it is with great confidence that I can say it is the bottle situation and not the Daddy situation.

He just doesn't want it. No impostor for my boy.

With this in mind, I think you'll agree traditional bonding was tough. Until just recently.

"Truck, truck, motorcycle, truck."

At almost 6 months of age, my son appears to have been teething for the last 5 ¾ months. Hardly an hour goes by when he doesn't have something the size of his fist stuck in his mouth, and he isn't drooling. When one tooth violently erupted from his lower gums last week, we hoped for a small respite from his incessant gnawing. And in fact, we got one.

For about an hour and a half.

Then the realization must have dawned on him that he still had 31 teeth waiting to stretch the boundaries of his gum line. This one bright spot enabled my brave young son to start his teething once again with renewed vigor.

It was during one of these drooling, gumming, runny nosed bouts while I was pacing the floor with our little trooper thrown over my shoulder, looking for that perfect something to take away the monumental discomfort in his mandible. I was trying to finish my lunch of leftover pizza. My wife was on the phone, so it was up to me to see if I could fulfill his urgent needs.

We went up the hall and back again. We passed through the living room and dashed into the dining room. We sat at the sweater chest, looked out the window and called out the passing travelers.

"Truck, truck, car, car, car."

For a few minutes, he seemed to enjoy the activity and motion just beyond our front yard gate.

"Van, van, bus, truck, truck, car."

His interest was fleeting however, and the passing Harley club didn't settle well.

"Motorcycle, motorcycle, motorcycle, motorcycle, motorcycle, motorcycle, motorcycle, motorcycle, motorcycle, motorcycle, motorcycle, motorcycle, motorcycle, motorcycle, motorcycle."

As I finished my first piece of pizza, I had the good fortune to be struck by a bolt of sheer inspiration. I pulled my son's fist, forearm and elbow out of his mouth and in its place, I wedged a burnt, solid, raw-hide rod of pizza crust. Within seconds he had quieted down, and he's now settled into the crook of my arm looking up into my eyes. With that special look, he lets me know he now feels secure.

"Car, car, car, car."

It took me six months to realize he was, in fact, my son, and what he needed to bond with me was just a little male bonding. To share in the masculine words of automobiles and to partake in the manly food of cold pizza. For the last 15 or 20 minutes we've been sitting on the sweater chest in our dining room, looking out at the highway passing, content to be in each other's company. A father and his son.

"Truck, truck ... Rrrrrr Veeeeeee!"

May, 1994

My Wife's Story

The story I'm telling today does not belong to me, though I wish it did. This anecdote belongs to my wife.

For two years my daughter was an only child. Her little brother came along after that. He is only five months old, and while he is doing an enviable job of taking parental attention away from his sister, he still has a ways to go before he fulfills his potential as a playmate.

My wife has had the good fortune to be able to stay at home with both of them since my son's birth. I have had the misfortune of having to return to work, so we can continue to put food on the table. I have relinquished my parenting experiences to be limited to weekday evenings and weekends. For the most part, my children's lives during the week are a mystery to me.

As I said, this is my wife's story.

My daughter has a favorite video with a scene that depicts two girls having a pillow fight. Goodness knows how many times she has seen this video and this particular scene. Every time she sees it, it's as if it were the first time. When the first pillow is thrown a deep and hardy chuckle begins inside her. By the end of the pillow fight she is in raging hysterics, barely able to breath. The Three Stooges couldn't do better.

One day last week after a somewhat hectic morning, my wife put our daughter down for a nap. When she finally got our son to sleep, she hoped to have a minute or two to complete some of her tasks around the house. Walking down the hall, she heard some noise coming from our daughter's room. We always leave her door open just a crack when she is sleeping. I think it's comforting for both my daughter and my wife. When my wife peeked through the crack, she watched our daughter stand her stuffed bunny up in front of her, give the bunny a good pummeling with her pillow and shriek with joy.

After the third attack, my wife entered the room, picked up bunny, pillow and blanky and said, "Honey, it's time for a nap. If bunny is keeping you awake, I can put him on the changing table."

With that, my daughter's bottom lip began to pucker ever so slowly, and tears began to fill her eyes. Something had to be done quickly before that lip's solo debut became a full chorus with the Philharmonic.

Without hesitation, my wife laid on the bed between her and the blue mesh guard rail that prevents our darling from falling off the bed in her sleep. She put the pillow under our daughter's head and tucked bunny to her side under the blanky. She told our daughter again that it was nap time and suggested a song to help her sleep.

"Let's sing 'Baby Beluga.'" Ever since our daughter was born, this tune had always relaxed her and she knew it.

"No!" she said with her palms stretched out. She knew that Baby Beluga would be the end for her. "Stop!" she pleaded.

But in a soft and comforting voice my wife began to sing, "Baby Beluga in the deep blue sea, swim so wild and you swim so free..."

By the end of the song, my wife and daughter were lying face to face. Their noses almost touching. My wife softly patted our little girl's back while my daughter patted her mother's.

No one's really sure how long the patting lasted. I don't think either knows who fell asleep first. I don't think it really matters. In the end they both got what they truly wanted. Comforting time with each other.

We get a monthly magazine with our diaper service. In it there is a column written by a stay at home dad who chronicles his life and his children's development as his wife goes off to work. In the last issue, he talks of a night when he rocked his five-month-old to sleep. With each rock he was able to look one year into their future. On his twenty-first rock he saw his little angel starting a life of her own while leaving his behind. He held his baby to his chest and wondered where that newborn had gone to.

I know that the twenty first rock is not far away for my children or for myself. It only emphasizes that this is still my wife's story.

I wish I could make it mine before the rocking ends.

May, 1994

Seals Like Me

There is nothing that is as inspiring and able to fill one's heart with hope for our crazy world, as there is when you witness language dawning upon the crest of a two-year-old's mind. When the sheer excitement of thoughts are transferred to the unbridled ecstasy of communication.

My daughter is almost three now. She has been speaking for quite awhile. She is comfortable with words, and sentences are no longer new. For the past few months or so, I have been able to see that language has taken hold of her and she has embraced it with a passion. The words come to her at an easy pace, but her thoughts are fired from a cannon.

I simply can not think of a sweeter melody than that of our daughter proudly trying to harness her ideas with this lasso of language.

Earlier this evening, I was lying on my daughter's bed and had just finished reading her a couple of bedtime stories. I was telling her about our plans for the next few days. Grandpa was coming to visit tomorrow, and the next day we were all going down to spend a few days by the ocean.

"At the beach," I told her. "You'll see lots of sand. There will be seagulls and little crabs. We'll also see the ocean. It has lots of water, and you can swim in it."

I told her that we would go to the zoo one day, to a park on another, but always we would have the biggest of sandboxes and the ocean to play in. Throughout it all my daughter listened with wide eyes and a broad smile. Occasionally, she would repeat a word or phrase that found an especially fertile spot to be planted in her mind.

When we finished, we shared a kiss and said good night. I went out of her room and took my seven-month-old son from his mother so she would have her chance to share in our daughter's dreams. I listened outside the door.

"Mamma," my daughter started. "Papa come and he bring a bathing suit and we go to beach and see boats and zoo and sand and I wear bathing suit and see seals and you wear suit too and pool and papa come tomorrow and see seals and there's monkeys and zebras and ocean and whales but they won't bite. And there will be bears but I don't want to see bears. And we'll see boats and a park and see seals and see papa and seals."

She then paused for a brief time, and after some reflection, she finished. "Seals don't bite... seals like me."

And I could only stand there in the hallway with my skin tingling and my heart pounding, caught up in the excitement of this song. It was then that I realized that I needed to start packing.

Our future was to be a full one, and we should all be excited.

July, 1994

Thanksgiving

During the past eleven months, there were times that I wondered when an evening might close and if I would ever make it to the end of the week. I would wake in the morning and shudder to see another never ending eighteen hours ahead before I'd have the chance to see my pillow again. A month on the calendar appeared to be a lifetime or two into the future.

It is November and my son was born almost one year past. I now sit and wonder where all those torturous days and nights have gone to. It has all passed so quickly.

At my son's first day of day care, he was the youngest infant enrolled. All the children's names and birth dates were put on paper plates that beam with hand drawn happy faces. These plates hung on the nursery wall with the youngest on one end while progressing in age to the other.

Such a short time ago, his name hung on the very right. Two months ago at an open house, he was second from the left. Last week his happy face came down. He is now a toddler.

When my daughter was born, our lives were filled with the busyness that a baby can bring to new parents. We easily settled into the role of raising an only child. In all honesty, she is and has always been an easy girl.

My son, in contrast, is a normal baby. He has provided us with a whole host of challenges that we hadn't encountered with our daughter. His birth brought to our home not just the diapering, feeding and burping of a baby, but it also brought colic that echoed through our happy abode from 10PM to 2AM for three and a half months. In addition, we embraced a two-year-old daughter who found herself competing with a little brother who was equipped with a set of lungs the size of the Pacific North West.

There were times when the thought of another eighteen years seemed terminal.

During these months I have been reminded time and again to try to enjoy the good moments we have. Friends and family tell me our children will quickly grow up and my memories will grow dim.

"I know," I would say to myself. "But they've been crying for three hours."

And now I am in November. I am sitting in our hall, and I wonder where my babies have gone to. My back is to the wall, and I listen to children in the next room. They are playing with a toy stove. They busily mix and stir and check with each other to make sure that just the right ingredients are added.

"One teaspoon," my daughter states.

"Cracra," my son replies.

"Burgers?"

For a few minutes there are no "Gimme"s, no "Mine"s, no shrieks through clenched fists. There is only a kitchen that is filled with the sounds of happy play.

These are the times I can't forget. The times that will get me through the next eleven months and the next eleven teething episodes. Time passes too quickly. While I am sitting in our hall perhaps my daughter will start chronicling her shopping list on our kitchen cabinets, and maybe my son will crawl into my lap while popping cat food into his mouth like chocolate bonbons.

These are all things that I am thankful for this November.

Before my peace can be shattered and our evening takes a different turn, my daughter pokes her head around the corner into the hall and says, "Daddy, we have muffins for you."

November, 1994

Holiday Magic

We received the gift from my wife's sister. It was a simple gift, and it came from the heart. She avoided the commercialness that is so prevalent in the Yuletide of today. What Helen gave to our family was a collection of memories. Memories that our family shared in the past, and memories that we will all continue to participate in in the future.

What we received was a photo album. And in this album were pictures that chronicled my wife's family from the time her parents were married to the present. Three hundred and forty six separate memories individually hand selected and displayed for those of us who remember today and for those who will be visiting tomorrow.

The first thing we did when the album was unwrapped was to gather round and wander our way through the past forty years. We laughed at how young Bill and Sue were when they got married. We chuckled at the 70's "Farrah" do my wife had in high school. We admired the white gelding that carried two little girls into the untamed frontier. I cried inside when we held the picture of my wife as a two year old next to the one taken of my daughter just last year. They looked like twins that were separated by a span of 30 years.

I glanced to my wife and marveled at the person she had become. I turned to my daughter and wondered where that baby girl was that posed in overalls only one year ago.

I'm confident that these memories are with us always. They are stored in our minds next to the first telephone number we memorized, or right by that first kiss. Often however, that is just where we store them. Pictures are what knock down the cobwebs, blow off the dust, and set them back to the forefront.

Our cerebral coffee table if you will.

I don't know how many hours Helen put into this album. From the large box under the end table, she put an album together for my wife, one for her brother and one for herself. It was truly a labor from her heart. I don't know how she could have shared the pictures evenly, making sure that each got their fair share of time gone by. It is the full spirit of the holidays crammed into a green three ring binder whose cover shines under a golden embossed crown. "Photos" is what it says.

But it held much more.

It was the love and intimacy we sometimes fail to remember during these hectic days of December. And though it was given to us by my sister-in-law, it was my three-year-old daughter who gave to us the magic of this season.

A day or so later, my daughter called to me and asked me to look at the pictures with her. There was something special she had to tell me. She turned to a picture of the day my wife and I married. It was the one where my wife and her father were sharing a final moment. She was in white lace and a wreath of flowers set upon her hair.

"Daddy!' my daughter said. "Daddy come look!" And then she whispered through eyes of passion, "Mommy is a princess."

The holidays are for the children. The magic is for them. It is theirs to cherish, theirs to hold, and perhaps, theirs to dream. I am blessed to love the princess that was photographed so many years ago. I am also blessed to hold on my lap another princess. One who is generous enough to share a little of her Yuletide magic with me.

December, 1994

My Sleeping Son

There is a peaceful contentedness you get when holding a sleeping angel in your arms. A sense of tranquility that melts into your chest and sweetens your soul. That taste will linger with you long after that cherub has gone.

My daughter is a little over 3. She is a self-professed big girl now. I'm no longer allowed to rock her off to her dreams. My son is a year old. With him, I know my days are numbered. Rarely do I get to hold him as he sleeps in my arms.

I try to cherish those times when I can. Often, long after he has fallen asleep, I find myself looking down at him. I want to drink him in to remember that sweet flavor of a 1-year-old.

When I glance down upon him, I wonder where that newborn, of a year past, has gone to. I try to see if there is anything left of him in those resting eyes and pursed lips. I do this for myself. I also look for the boy who is growing in him. The man he will become. And this I do for him.

For now anyway, he is the one that I talk to during these quiet times. I tell him the things that I would like for him.

I tell him to sleep well, and I wish only good dreams. I apologize for the chin I have given him, and I boast of the hair he got from his mother. I tell him to play soccer and not football. I tell him to ride horses and not motorcycles. I tell him that he might be a veterinarian some day.

I tell him to stay out of sales.

I tell him to grow strong and honest. I tell him to seek knowledge and not hide from it. I tell him it's important to think things through for himself and not to follow the crowd.

I want him to be careful when he selects those who are to be friends, and even more careful when he selects those who are not to be. I tell him to measure his successes by his whole worth. I tell him to enjoy life, to look for the happiness he already has.

I want him to be independent, to be able to start his own family and raise them wherever he finds happiness. And in doing so, I tell him to break my heart.

I tell him to live life for himself and not for me.

I tell him I don't want him to get hurt.

I tell him these things now because I know my time is limited. In a blink of an eye, he will no longer want to sleep in my arms. In another blink, he won't have time to be interested in the things I wish to share. I want the time to come when he will listen to himself. I can even envision the time when I will be asking him for his help and guidance.

These are some of the things I say to the young boy in my arms; to the man he will become.

But when it has become late, and I'm content that enough has been said, I lay my angel in bed for the night. Looking down I savor him. I kiss his forehead and once again, I wonder.

Where is that newborn of just a year past?

February, 1995

Living in the Past

A picture of a fireman holding a baby. It fills the TV screen. It covers the front page. It burns within my heart.

There is so much that I take for granted in my life. Family, friendship, good health, the prospect of tomorrow. Occasionally, an event comes along that gives me a sharp nudge and reminds me that all of these need to be enjoyed and savored while I still have them.

It can be something as innocent as watching my daughter look to the clouds while talking of an old mare who long ago left our mortal soil. Or it can be something as simple as a picture of a fireman carrying a baby.

It tells me that what we have now, in a breath of an instant, could be gone forever.

I am reminded of a magazine I looked through a few years ago. It contained some turn of the century daguerreotypes of children who were close to death, and of others who had just passed on. Those near death were posed in bed, wearing a fresh, clean nightshirt. Most held a favorite belonging. Those who had died were dressed in their Sunday best and propped in a pose of contentedness. One girl, sat in a chair while she held a flower in her hand. Her head was tilted down and eyes were half-closed as if she were looking at the flower. A drop of blood rested on her lip just under her nose.

I had studied all the pictures before I read any of the text. I thought it odd that both photographer and family, would have the same morbid fascination that would compel them to capture such a painful moment.

What I found in the words, however, was quite different. The author had pointed out, that in that era, photographers were few and photographs were expensive. For most of the children shown on those pages, these were the only images ever taken. The only remnant for those left behind to embrace after young lives had faded.

Today, I look over and see our camcorder resting on the shelf. I know the battery needs charging and won't be ready for that next milestone achieved by my daughter or son. A memory that might be destined to slip away and washed from my mind.

A camera is sitting next to it, quietly waiting for film.

At times, it has been suggested that I live too much in the past. I focus too much on memories, and on things that I have had. "Look towards tomorrow," I've been told. "Look for the joy to come." As if there is a line, that moves forward with me and bisects my life. Something that can clearly separate everything behind from everything ahead.

But to me, it can't be that clear.

My past has been good. Happy memories are plentiful. The birth of my children. Summer days playing soccer in the school yard. A beautiful girl in pigtails. But I have pain too. The death of a friend. An injury from youth that haunts me still. Writing a eulogy for my mother.

Perhaps, I embrace my past to make sure that I don't take too much for granted. I cling to my memories to remind me of all the riches I have today.

So I go out and buy more film, and I charge the camcorder's battery. A simple photograph tells me to. You see, today, when I look at a picture of a fireman, I am reminded that tomorrow, in the breath of an instant, another young life may fade and another eulogy may need to be written.

April, 1995

First Overnight

"**B**rrsssdsssdsssdsssdssst!"

That's the sound my camera makes when it's rewinding film. Family law states it can only be rewound when you're about two snapshots into some special event or holiday.

"Brrsssdsssdsssdsssdssst," is what it says on Christmas morning.

"Brrsssdsssdsssdsssdssst," is what it says as a birthday cake is chorused into the room.

"Brrsssdsssdsssdsssdssst," is what it says on that warm day in spring when the three-ring pool is first filled.

It was a month or so ago when our friends, Rhonda and Allen, first invited our daughter to spend the night with their daughter, Jessika.

My wife and I have no family in the area. No relatives to send the kids to for an evening of quiet. No aunts or uncles. No grandparents. The only time my daughter had spent an evening away from my wife and I was when her brother was born. I think it's fair to say that that event ended with a little more of a jolt than my daughter had anticipated.

So, at 3 years of age, this was to be my daughter's first sleep over.

I felt I had to tread lightly to ensure I didn't shatter her trust when she took those first steps towards autonomy. The plan was to slowly break her into the "overnight" idea. I wanted to make sure it didn't turn into a traumatic event that could emotionally scar her for years.

I decided to lay the ground work early.

"Honey?" I asked with a voice brimming with gentleness. "Maybe, sometime you could spend the night at Jessika's and sleep at her house. Would you like to do that sometime?"

"Sleep at Jessika's?" she asked through a knitted brow. "Where would you and Mama sleep?"

"Well, Mama and I would sleep in our bed at home." I had to tell her the truth. She had to know we would be leaving her there alone. I knew the potential these words held and the damage they could do.

"Yeah!" she cried, jumping up and down and shaking her hands.

Her mile-wide smile gave her away. Only an experienced father could see through the walls she had built. Deep inside I knew she was fearstruck.

Okay, so I guess the real uncertainty rested with me and my wife. How could we guard our daughter when she was out of our reach? I mean, sure we had known Alan and Rhonda for years, even long before either of us had children. We knew they would be great, but she was still our little girl.

How could we protect her when she was almost seven miles away?

Eventually, the evening came when it was time to pack our daughter's Garfield backpack and roll up the Big Bird sleeping bag. We pulled some of her favorite books from the library, gathered Bunny Rabbit and a few other friends and slipped in a copy of the family photo we used for this year's Christmas card.

I opened the back door, and we headed for the garage.

I paused by the geraniums in the back yard. I wanted one more moment with my little girl. I knew when I picked her up the next morning she wouldn't be the same. I knew in less than 14 hours, she would be older and wiser. It was to be my daughter's first step away from me.

She was on her way to becoming a big girl.

I squatted down beside her, pushed her hair away from her face, and told her I wanted just one more. And then, with a tear in my heart, I pushed the button.

"Brrsssdsssdsssdsssdssst!"

April, 1995

No Time for Intimacies

We were at a party thrown by some old college friends when I realized that I was doomed. It was the type of party that five years ago would have lasted well into the morning hours. Fifteen years ago we would have toasted the crack of noon on the following day. But, that was before all of us had children. This was to be a "family" party, and I expected to be on our way home by 9:30, 10 o'clock at the latest.

By 8 o'clock, the other kids were being packed up with full diaper bags, three sets of sleepers, and a 12-pack of formula, everything needed to spend the night at Grandma and Grandpa's or Uncle Larry's. When they were kissed good night, their parents said, "Have fun. We'll see you tomorrow."

By 9, we were the only ones who still had our kids. Our friends had the whole evening and a morning of leisure to look forward to, but I still had to put my daughter to bed, schedule time for the 3 o'-clock feeding and pray for a wake up call no earlier then five.

That schedule hadn't changed for months, and there was nothing telling us the routine would be short lived. You see, that evening occurred years ago, but things haven't changed much since then. The only time my wife and I were able to spend a whole night away from kids was the night my son was born.

I'm reminded of a joke that Wally Kaiser, a retired traveling pen salesman, told me on the eve of his first becoming a grandfather. The joke considers how soon amorous relations can be renewed after childbirth. Let's just say contrary to Wally's conventional wisdom, it was not the most ideal opportunity for a romantic interlude.

Today, years later, there still isn't time for us to nurture the more intimate aspects of a relationship. First, I'm exhausted from the first cry for breakfast to the soft wump of my head hitting the pillow 20 hours later. Second, whatever free time there is, is usually spent piloting the family wagon from swim lessons to the park, to dance lessons, to shopping, and finally, to the 100 birthday parties that happen each week. And when a spare minute can be found to savor each other on a more spiritual level, one undoubtedly whispers the phrase that can cool a burning passion faster then Desitin douses diaper rash.

"We might wake the kids."

I'll say it again. I'm doomed.

Tonight the family is at the Discovery Zone. The DZ, as it's called, is an indoor playground with life-sized Habitrails connected by slides, net bridges and swingy things that you drop from. The Zone proprietors have recently fitted the entire play area with a super Power Ranger sound system that bounces all kinds of cool Power Ranger zaps, blips and fffthhhh sounds from one section to another.

It's approaching the closing hour and almost time to start thinking about getting the children home and in bed. My wife and I are in this giant room that is a sea of little plastic colored balls. I'm lying on my back trying to throw balls through a basketball hoop. My wife is sitting off to the side watching the kids play in another section. The red, blue and yellow balls of the play area are casting a provocative primary glow upon my wife's profile, and I roll over onto my side to get a better view of this radiant beauty. Most of the other families have left by now and a comforting hush has fallen over the Discovery Zone. Only an occasional Power Ranger fffthhhh is passed around the room.

You know, if we could find someone to take the kids. And if the lights were dimmed a little. And if they pumped some Barry Manilow into the super Power Ranger sound system ...

Geez! I am doomed!

July, 1995

Aunt Marilee

H *ola. Como esta? Bien, y tú? Muy bien. Donde está su casa?*
That's what I got out of seventh grade Spanish. Though I also took Spanish in eighth grade and as a freshman in high school, the only stuff that stuck is from seventh.

Feliz Navidad.

When college came along I was able to add to my vocabulary, but what little I did gather came from more of a social than academic setting.

Dos cervezas, por favor? Donde está el baño?

I regret not learning a second language when I had the time and the resources available. At 4 years of age, my daughter knows more Spanish than I did at 14, or 24, or 34 for that matter. Though she can't yet form sentences, she has a vast array of words stored in her vocabulary that are available at a moment's notice. She can count as high in Spanish as she can in English and sings along with *De Colores.*

Last spring, as my daughter and I were waiting in the doctor's reception area, a mother and two teen-aged daughters sat next to us. When their conversations started to float on the lyrical melodies of this Latin language, my daughter was overcome. "Daddy!" she shouted. "They are speaking Spanish!"

Not wishing to disturb the tranquil silence that quickly followed, I smiled and nodded my agreement to her. The younger of the trill-tongued, teen-aged daughters smiled too and asked my little *ángel* if she could speak Spanish.

My daughter nodded and in a barely audible voice started to whisper into her closed hand, *"Uno, dos, tres..."*

Another time when we were in a Japanese restaurant, my little girl grabbed my arm and pointed to a table of waitresses folding napkins. In a voice strained with restraint she whispered, "Daddy, they're not speaking Spanish."

Am I proud of my little linguist? *Sí.*

Am I bragging about the genius that is my princess? *Muy sí!* As with all things though, no reward comes painlessly. Her love for language comes not from me but from outside. A vulture that preys on innocents and pulls them from the tender loving arms of a father.

Every father has one. My rival is Aunt Marilee.

She isn't really an aunt. Rather, she is a friend who teaches with my wife. Spanish is what she teaches.

It started long ago. When my wife was pregnant, Marilee would speak to my daughter in utero. She was the first visitor my daughter had after her birth. Hers were two of the six hands that changed the first diaper.

Today, when Aunt Marilee visits, it is she who reads "The Iguana Brothers."

"Nobody got *flaco.* And nobody got *pálido.* And nobody's tail dropped off. *De veras.*"

It is Marilee who scours the Dr. Seuss Dictionary in Spanish "Scissors. *Las tijeras.* Snip, snip, snip." It is Marilee who brings to my daughter a linguistic diamond when all Daddy has is a lump of coal.

The other night after watching videos, my daughter asked Marilee to brush her teeth. A task generally done by Dad.

"Vamos a cepillo los dientes," Marilee crooned as she caressed cuspids. *"Los dientes blancos,"* she softly sang. *"Las perlas bonitas,"* she whispered. *"Tu lengua."*

I stood by and listened to her sing her song of love to my little girl, and I knew my daughter was lucky.

Every family has one, an aunt or uncle who is loved like no other. And to my daughter, Marilee is not just the gift of Spanish. A gift that I could never give her. She is a birthday ever new. She is the gift, the flowered paper, ribbon, and bow all wrapped in one. She is balloons and banners. Ice cream and cake.

Es cierto. Every family has one and ours is called Marilee. Really. *De veras!*

September, 1995

A Remembrance From Fall

On frosted fall mornings, the old truck would sit at the end of the drive. Its idle would be half-choked and sputtering until the I-block 6 was warmed. That's what he remembers about autumn.

The old white Ford rarely came out of the barn except on weekend mornings. And then it was only used to haul hay back from the Feed & Seed. The son would stand at the end of the cement waiting for his chance to ride inside this great whale. It would be just the three of them, a man, a boy, and a beat-up, old truck.

The truck's throaty thunder was due to a leaky muffler that when new, tamed this lion's roar to a purr. But that was before the son's time. The boy would only remember a white giant hollering out its invitation, raged and unmuffled.

When it was time, the father would lift the hood, drop the choke and slam the hood down again. Sometimes a second lift and slamming were necessary to seal the gaping mouth. Only then would Papa allow his son to climb onto the running board and wait for father's hands to lift him onto the seat.

The door would then be shut, and the boy would smile as the father's head bobbed over the dashboard's horizon around to the driver's side. Another door would shut, then gears would grind and with another roar from the engine, father, son and old friend would lurch into motion and crawl onto the highway.

The first half mile was taken slow. Back then there was only one stop sign on the way out of town. After that, the truck could be opened up to soar past the green fields and orchards.

In the winter months, the leaky muffler also meant that windows would be opened wide. The heater would be at full throttle sprinkling a pinch of warmth into the ice cold stream that rushed through the cab. Fertile smells of dairy and poultry were tinged with exhaust. A heady mixture that was sure to accent the day's adventure.

Once on their way, father and son would shout out songs above the shuddering rattles that surrounded them. Dramatic conversations were shouted about birds on barbed wire or cows in the mud. Everything was carried on at amplified levels so that it could be heard over the pumping pistons and the windows' gusting wind.

Sometimes they would simply listen to smooth melodies roughed from a 6-volt whine turned to full volume. Sometimes, they just sat and savored their journey.

The truck would eventually be backed into a barn that was filled with layered mountains of hay. On one side was the scent of spring piled to the rafters. Along another wall summer was neatly stacked.

The son would watch out the window as a man dropped bales from the peaks down into the truck. The father laid each bundle one on top of the other. When mountains were moved and hands were shook, the truck roared back to life. On the trip back, autumn was mixed with bits of alfalfa and oats swirling through the cab.

The journey home was slower then. The burden forced a steadier pace. The road's shoulder was hugged as sleek cars stirred leaves in passing winds. A swaying turn would bring them back to their drive.

Finally, a smiling son would watch out the window as spring and summer were stacked anew.

When the leaves begin to fall, he recalls the gleaming of a young boy standing at the end of the drive, waiting in anticipation of the roar to be held in the day's adventure.

That's what he remembers about autumn.

November, 1995

The Candy Land Cognitive Development Skills Assessment Test

Two blue.

I'm playing a game of Candy Land with my daughter. I just told her how I used to play the same game when I was a kid. Well almost the same.

Candy Land has changed over the years. A story now lays out a plot, and I don't seem to remember anything like that from the game of my youth. The whole object was to climb from treat to treat and get to the end first.

When I was young, the Candy Land that I played had special cards that were portrayed as actual treats. There was chocolate cake, lollipops, and the ever popular ice cream sandwich. Today, they have all been replaced by characters from a sweetened land that adequately fits their description. Princess Lolly from the Lollipop Woods, the evil Lord Licorice who has hidden King Kandy, and Grandma Nutt who lives in the Peanut Brittle House.

One green.

I should also note that Candy Land serves a different purpose for a child than it does for a parent. To a child it's a game to be enjoyed with family. To a parent, it is a way to evaluate a child's level of thinking, and determine what stage of development they've achieved.

It is in this spirit that I've developed the Candy Land Cognitive Development Skills Assessment Test, or what I affectionately refer to as the CLCDSAT.

Two orange.

Here's how it works. Everybody starts at the beginning of the trail. The object is to be the first one to arrive at King Kandy's Castle. The only way you can move is by drawing a card from the deck and following its simple directions; two greens, one red, or a face card, like Mr. Mint, where you jump ahead to that card's desired domain.

Okay? All good so far?

Now, let's say you're lucky enough to draw Queen Frostine. This enables you to blow by all of your competitors, and land a mere 30 spaces from Kandy's Castle. In the meantime, Mom and Dad are still struggling through Mr. Mint's Peppermint Forrest, which is precisely 93 squares back.

Victory is virtually assured.

Once a child reaches that level of development, it becomes clear that there is only one thing Candy Land has to offer a young supple mind that is yearning for learning. That is simply to teach this new thinker to cheat.

One green.

You don't believe me, do you?

Okay, mom and dad want junior to learn to shuffle and develop some fine motor skills. Right? Well, as soon as this little Mr. or Miss can put 2 and 2 together, Johnny or Janie has also figured that the odds of him or her winning can be greatly increased if they stack the deck.

Really! Slide in the beloved Ice Queen 3 cards down... Then it's Mom's turn... Dad's turn... Then... "HOLY COW! MOM, DAD! I DREW QUEEN FROSTINE! CAN YOU BELIEVE THAT?!"

It is my belief that this landmark falls on or around the fourth birthday. And once your darling has discovered CL's simple message, you can assume that A) Your child has embraced a higher level of critical thinking and has embarked on an unstoppable quest for knowledge B) He or she has a future in politics, or C) It's time to stop playing Candy Land for money.

One purple.

Tonight I've creamed my daughter twice already. She didn't even get out of the Gingerbread Plum Trees. She never had a chance. I know my days are numbered though. Her fourth birthday is in a few weeks and next game, she wants to shuffle.

Whoa, Honey! I drew Queen Frostine! Can you believe that?!

December, 1995

Two Pictures

In our home there is a photograph of a young man in the woods. He is sitting on a rock, wearing cowboy boots, jeans, and a Levi jacket. A little boy is standing next to him. He hugs his father's arm while his head rests on daddy's shoulder. He is wearing a red baseball jacket, peppered with the emblems of baseball teams across the country.

In another room sits a picture of a man in a cap wearing a t-shirt and a backpack. In the pack sits another boy whose head is happily resting by daddy's shoulder.

The two photographed men appear to be the same age. The sons might be a few years apart. In both pictures, however, the love that can be seen knows no years. The soft and gentle pleasures of fatherhood have rounded both men to a level of contentment that will remain unequaled.

The first picture is of my father and myself when we took a walk through one of the many forests of my childhood. It was taken some 30 years back. The second is of me and my son playing the spectators at one of the endless circles of parades he seems to be so fond of.

A father's love is often found in surprising ways. My father's mother died when I was 22. She was the last of my grandparents to pass away. It is a custom in our faith that when a loved one is buried, the family walks a path between the remaining mourners. My father being the eldest was the first to walk that course. I as the youngest was the last.

My father remained stolid through to the end with head held high. My stoicism faded early. Part way down my passage, my father approached, hugged me and whispered not to cry, that it would hurt him too much if I did. At the time I had heard what he said, but, now I know, I couldn't possibly have known what he meant.

Not until I had children of my own.

With this, I wish to retell two of my favorite quotes. The first is from the Talmud: "A father's love is for his children and the children's love for their children."

It wasn't until nine years after my grandmother's passing, when my daughter was born, that I knew how much my father loved me. A love so strong it hurt more for my father to see his son grieving than his own loss had pained him. A love I can still see in the same man sitting in the woods 30 years earlier.

The second quote reads "What a father says to his children is not heard by the world, but it will be heard by posterity." I have looked at that man on the rock for many years now, and I can still hear the words he holds in his heart. And when I look to the little boy at the parade, I can see it is true. My son will hear those very words of love I have heard for over 30 years.

They will be heard by posterity.

January, 1996

Daddy All Gone

It was a Monday evening and my wife, daughter and son were sitting around the dining room table. Dinner was just about finished and a lull had settled over the normally hectic room. My 2-year-old son was sitting in his highchair. He slowly lowered his head until his cheek was resting on the tray. After a moment he whispered, to no one in particular, "My daddy all gone."

Events in my life have forced me into something I thought would never happen. Men the world over have shared similar tales: work keeping them away from their families for months or even years on end. My own father lived in another country for a time, so he could provide for his wife and children.

Perhaps I have become a victim of fatherhood.

I have been working away from my family for a few weeks now. From Monday to Friday my duration is spent 172 miles north of them. Friday night we are united again, but only for two days. I am a weekend commuter.

Fortunately, my situation won't last so long. Shortly my family will be here in Chico with me. Meals, bedtime stories, and baths will be times spent together. Week-night wrestling will shortly resume. Within a month I will be pushing two swings as the mid-week sun glowingly paints a dusk-colored sky.

Six weeks at the outside.

In the mean time, I live in a house that is not my home. There are paintings on the refrigerator and pictures on the table, but the walls here are hollow. Silence echoes from room to room, and I long to hear little voices singing, shouting, crying. The view out my back door is vacant of slides and swings and chalk-colored walk ways.

I know life is no easier three hours south. Though my 4-year-old daughter knows I will return to her on Friday, from a Monday point of view that might be a week, a month, or a lifetime away. To my son, however, if I'm not home for dinner, I am simply gone.

A week and a half later my son was playing with a teacher at day care. Her name is Heather. Although she is a young woman and just starting life for herself, she is as gentle and tender with her charges as if they were her own. She was tickling my son this particular afternoon, and they filled the room with laughter. When they had both come up for breath, she held my young boy and said that she loved him. The smile slipped from my son's lips, and he looked to Heather and said, "My daddy loves me."

My wife knows this is hard on me. She secrets more away then what she reveals. But I know it is trying on her too. Routines are broken, and rituals have been uprooted. New things can be a caution to our children.

She tells me the first couple of days are rough. Our children don't understand why Dad suddenly goes away. She also says the two days before I return are difficult. The uniqueness of the week's adventure has faded.

That only leaves Wednesday.

I speak to all each night on the phone. I ask how their day has been. My son always responds, "Pre good. I play wit Hetter." I remind them I will be home in a few days. I tell them I love them.

When the phone is hung up and I face a quiet house, I am reminded of how much I miss happy smiles and sad pouts, maddening screams and ticklish giggles. I close my eyes and I think of how we'll be together. How we'll sit down for dinner and say our thanks. I can see the time when I will lean my head over ever so slowly and touch the little hands that I have missed, and whisper into their precious hearts, "Daddy all back."

February, 1996

KITE DAY

Last week, Kite Day was observed in my neck of the woods. It was a day where community joined in the joyous celebration of life packaged in bits of paper and string. Where families gathered to take off shoes, run through the grass and grab a small piece of wind to call their own.

The events began at noon, and though we started packing a full week and a half in advance, we still rolled into the designated park precisely one hour late, SFT (Standard Family Time). It should be noted a half-gazillion people made it there before us, and already had two and a half-gazillion kites in the air.

We staked ourselves an open patch of grass in the midst of all the excitement and found ample wind for our day's event. The family sat down in a small semi-circle, and the kites were brought out for assembly.

Within minutes my wife and 4-year-old daughter had Aladdin and Jasmine soaring. A moment later, Goofy, Donald and Mickey were stretching for the clouds with my son as their anchor. Another 20 seconds along, my 2-year-old boy was shrieking with elation as he let go of the string. To his further delight, I madly dashed through a forest of rooted kite strings all the while singing a cheerful little ditty that went something like this: "Sorry ... Excuse me ... Oooops ... Sorry about that."

You need to keep in mind I spent well over $2.67 for this kite, and I intended to get every penny's worth out of it.

The string eventually wrapped around the lines of about five families down wind. I was able to retrieve our flier after the wind had sheared my line and Goofy, Mickey and Donald haplessly tumbled groundward.

It was precisely at this moment I discovered Kite Day could have been even better if it wasn't for all that kite string. When the kite, the remaining line and my son had all been reunited, I spent the next 20 minutes alternately trying to repair the broken string and untangle my little boy from all of his unabashed enthusiasm.

With that completed, my son happily started off to find some other's web to wind himself in.

It is idle string that truly is the devil's playground.

On the bright side, however, the entire crowd just ran right along with the hundreds of mishaps that mishappened all around. If one could have paused from their own personal disasters for just a moment, they might have seen a half dozen other fathers chasing down kites that got away. And when lines got crossed or tangled, most everyone enjoyed a kindred chuckle as the diligent task of untangling began.

Even the guy 20 yards in front of me didn't sour as our Goofy swooped and dived, nearly decapitating his child, before it drilled into the side of his head. I actually saw him giggle while he dug bits of plastic and paper out of his ear.

By the end of the day, people milled through the park happily fatigued from running, ducking, and untangling, and pooped from their efforts of looking up and then looking down. Cheeks were tender from the day's smiling. Hearts and hair were tousled about and left the better for it. I had different expectations when I had arrived earlier in the day. A simple field for flight is what was sought, but a winsome kingdom filled with laughter is what was found.

Not bad for a few sheets of paper and a bit of string.

March, 1996

Value in a Yard Sale

Everything has value. No matter how small or inanimate an object may be, it has to have some value. Even at a yard sale.

We purged ourselves a few weeks ago with this ritualistic cleansing of the home/college account fundraiser. Each time we have such an event I'm amazed at the incredible deals garage sale shoppers scoff at.

"I've never seen a vacuum like that," one senior shopper said. It was an ageless black Hoover bordering antique. "My mother probably has though," she added.

"Well," I told her. "I can make you a heck of a deal on it. Just think how much your mom would love you if you bought it for her. Imagine the flood of warm memories she'd have just by the sight of it. Those kind of memories are priceless, you know."

"I don't think so, Honey. My mother's been dead for 13 years."

That's how things go at yard sales. A perfectly collectible vacuum that should sell for $5 is let go for 50 cents. Or worse, put back in the garage on Monday. Even a full set of World Book Encyclopedias from 1962 (Some day, man could walk on the moon!) was passed by.

Really, everything has some value.

A steady parade of thrifty shoppers made their way through our yard that day. Many of them left with plastic bags stuffed with somethings for nothing. Others entered our yard veiled in silence only to shatter our hearts with, "The folks down the street have three typewriters that they can't give away."

Our last shopper established the day's defining moment.

It was the end of the day, when we had cleared at least $16.49. I saw a young man walking across the street. He was dressed in a worn shirt and jeans. A baseball cap covered half combed hair. He was followed by a bone thin, black and brown dog that managed to stay 10 to 15 paces behind.

He crossed and entered our yard. The dog stayed at the end of the driveway.

After he browsed some, he picked up two perfectly good flashlights we had to reduce to 25 cents. He glanced at a table that held our children's outgrown clothes and shyly thumbed through a pastel collection of diaper wraps. He asked how much they cost.

"Twenty five cents," I told him. They cost us almost $8 a piece.

"Do they fit newborns?"

I told him some did and showed him the tags and how they were sized. "Do you have a newborn?" I asked.

"One on the way," he said in a voice strained with confidence.

"Do you know when it's due?"

"In December."

"Really! My son was born in December. What day?"

"I don't know exactly. I know it's sometime in mid-December." His eyes rarely met mine.

With a wrap under one arm, he went to another table, put down the flashlights and started to dig around in his jeans pocket. When he returned, he picked out three more wraps, two white and one yellow. The remaining were all pink. He gave me a dollar in change.

"Do you know if it's a boy or girl?" I asked.

"No I don't," he said. "I kinda hope for a boy though."

He paused for a moment, reached into his pocket and gave me his last 25 cents. "I guess it could be a girl," he considered as he picked out a pink wrap.

"Well, I have a girl and a boy, and either way they're great," I mentioned. Then added, "My son never minded the pink ones. Why don't you take them all."

And with his small purchase, the young man turned back to the road.

Everything has value. Even at a yard sale.

April, 1996

A Tale of Two Fathers

My thoughts this afternoon flow as a staged play. In this production, two fathers are fighting to protect the future for their children. Both are pounding their fists. Neither are listening to each other. If I'm not careful, by the time the curtain has dropped, my heart may very well be ripped in two.

The script for this drama is simple. A 16-year-old boy has fired a handgun above a crowd at a public park. He has been charged and found guilty; the sentence pronounced. The two fathers take polarizing positions on the severity of the punishment. The first says that, for the security of the community, harshness is required. An example must be made.

The second argues that though a crime has been committed, in reality, it was a thoughtless mistake with the good fortune of hurting no one. Harshness in this circumstance, could cripple a young life.

In this cerebral performance I have the misfortune of casting myself in the roles of both fathers. I am forced to play opposite myself with equal amounts of emotion and conviction.

Currently, my theater has paused for intermission. I am nervously pacing backstage waiting for the second act to begin. It is here I find my menace. As I wait for the lights to dim and the curtain to rise, I will allow you a glimpse of what our script holds.

As a father I want to protect my children from elements in society that are less than desirable. I stand up and say I want the innocence of my home protected. A young man has committed a violent crime and as the responsible party, he needs to be held accountable. A position needs to be clearly and firmly posted that his actions will not be tolerated.

Harshness is not what I want. Harshness is what I demand.

As another father, I now look to my own son. I know who he is, and I know his personality. I know well the stock that he is made of. I try to look ahead in his life and see the kind of individual he will become.

Will he make mistakes? Of course. Will he make poor decisions? Yes. Could those mistakes have the potential to hurt or kill? Unfortunately, they could.

Who hasn't acted out in anger, frustration, or fear only to be quickly sobered by the realization of what could have happened? Who hasn't raced through a stop light, or hastily cut through traffic?

If no one is hurt or harmed from such misdeeds, should a son have to pay for such mistakes? Unequivocally yes. Should he have to pay so painfully as to cost him his future?

Of course this is not a play. It's not a story staged with dramatic flair and captivating dialogue. It is real and has been played out in a theater of community. There are no directors, no actors, no foley grips.

The participants are quite real.

The repercussions will be quite real also. And whether they are good or bad, like a drop in a pond, their ripples will spread and flow throughout our community.

Like many, I am just one father who has been forced to play both roles. Like many, I have the conviction and the passion for both parts. Like many, I am now nervously pacing.

The lights are dimming, and I have taken my place on stage. As the curtain begins to rise I open my script to reassure myself. I turn to the beginning of the second act, and I find no comfort, for the pages are blank.

April, 1996

The Arcade

I have found, in my brief tenure as a father, that life's lessons can be found in the most undiscriminating places. Perhaps on a hike or at the beach or even while chewing sausage and cheese, it is possible to be struck by that golden bolt of lightning.

We have this arcade/restaurant for children in our area. An ad in the paper said that with a purchase of a large pizza, we would receive 100 game tokens absolutely free. Well sure, it's not Ed McMahon knocking on the front door, but 100 free tokens? That should work out to nearly a life time supply.

We met Paul and Beverly there with their 2 kids, Eric and Whitney. Being old arcade veterans themselves, Paul and Bev were kind enough to show us the ropes.

When we arrived, they had already claimed 2 tables. One was for the adults. The other, we had hoped, would be for the children. Instead, it held only 4 single slices of pizza on 4 plates. As the evening wore on, those 4 slices grew cold and lonely as they patiently waited to be eaten. By the time we had left, vultures were seen circling over the untouched pizza.

Looking back, those 4 slices were like an eerie still life painted on a formica canvas. It could have been titled; Lost Nutrition Stolen by Wack-A-Mole.

Most of the room was filled with slot sucking demons that would gladly steal your soul for the taste of a single token. My son was personally taken with the black railroad train and its electronic whistle.

"I think I can. I think I can. I think I can," my son and his new found locomotive friend endlessly chugged. After each trip he would circle the little choo choo unable to comprehend their lack of progress.

My four-year-old daughter, now able to travel in the faster circles, finished her evening following Eric and Whitney.

"Daddy, Daddy!" she screamed. "You have to come play the Barbie game with me!"

Barbie and Ken race opposing Jet Skis across the table. As participants, my daughter and I were to drop 2 tokens in the slot.

Barbie handily beat Ken in the first 15 seconds. It should be noted that Barbie had unfairly benefited from the advantages of affirmative action. Even at the starting line, Barbie had a nose and a half lead without the first token even being dropped. Plus, Ken wasn't even holding on to the handle bars. His arms were almost straight up in the air!

I mean, how can a guy be expected to race when he's not even holding on to the handle bars? That's what I want to know.

By evening's end, Paul and I were the only ones sitting at our little pizza table. My wife was off racing Barbie, and Bev was off chasing Whitney. Within a few moments, Paul's 8-year-old son Eric arrived. In his hand were 736 tickets that he had won from the assorted games. When totaled, these tickets could be used to buy toys displayed at a counter.

"Dad?" Eric asked as he held his bounty high. "Do you think I should buy something with all these, or should I save them for later?"

Eric's eyes quickly locked on his father.

Paul blinked once.

I froze and looked hard to Paul for some inkling.

Paul blinked again.

It was here that the golden bolt of wisdom appeared. Here that I discovered a truth that needed to be learned before I could face another tomorrow as a father.

"Well," Paul slowly stated. "If I were you," and then he paused. "I would really have to think about that one."

You see, the value of an answer is not in the giving but in its discovery.

June, 1996

ABCs

Today is another day to be recorded in my calendar of family. Another benchmark to be acknowledged. A milestone, if you will, that has been surpassed in the young life of my daughter.

"Daddy," my 4-year-old shyly grinned as she sat in my lap. "I'm learning my ABCs."

And with that I proudly whittle a notch in the bannister of life. It is with broad strokes I inscribe this image into the cross grains and burl of our sometimes swirling existence. I carve it deep and true, and when I'm done, I give myself a moment's pause and sing it out loud.

"My daughter has started to learn her ABCs."

For two years my little girl has been reciting the alphabet with ever increasing enunciation and clarity. Until recently, however, those very letters have held no meaning to her. They've only been a song sung on sunny afternoons while holding hands on a front porch swing.

Today things are different. She somehow has gotten the taste for consonants on her tongue and has savored the heady scent of vowels. It is her first reach for a key which will unlock a bottomless chest of treasures.

I'm not telling you this to boast of any super-cerebral prowess my little angel possesses. Nor am I bragging of any accelerated stages of language acquisition. To me, she has simply taken her first steps down a road I hope she will embrace with heart as well as head.

It is here I find the beauty. Here, I find the calm serenity of the purling stream. Here, I find the sharpness of a canyon's edge. My daughter has taken a step towards a journey that will never end for her. A trip we have all embarked on, towards a conclusion which we'll never know.

To me it is not just the rudimentaries of making marks on a page. It doesn't stop there. Today, my daughter may only be learning to draw the letters of the alphabet. Tomorrow she will make words. And very soon she will rope them into sentences. In my mind, it is all just learning ABCs.

I can see my daughter bobbing along, stumbling and tumbling down this twisting path. I see cartwheels and somersaults, back flips and pirouettes. I envision a passage for her that has no destination and an enchantment that has no end.

Each time we put pen to paper or touch a keyboard's pad, we're just learning new uses for our 26 little friends. Each time we pick something up to read, the very symbols we have taken for granted for so long, hold a fresh and new meaning for us. I'm not referring only to magazines or newspaper columns, but letters and notes and the hand scrawled "I love you"s found on lunch box napkins.

These are the reasons that, today, a landmark has been made. And this is why I have written my sentiments for all the world to see. Today my daughter has started a beautiful penned garden by planting the seeds of prose. Today life's harvest has begun.

May, 1996

Another Tuesday Night

It is a Tuesday night, and I am sitting in front of my keyboard. This is the night that I have set aside to write the columns you read here. It is the time that my family and I have dedicated towards an activity that is sometimes a pleasure and sometimes something a little less.

Tonight falls into the latter.

For a good portion of this "night away", I have stared blankly at an unmerciful monitor that has unfailingly stared back. I futz through a baggie of little wooden animals that twice a year hold candles on birthday cakes.

My children run up and down the hall as if it were a 3 foot wide Dakota plain, overrun with stampeding buffalo. When the bathtub is full, I walk into the bathroom and peruse the room, the tub, the bath toys, anything I can for any scrap of a story to start with.

For a moment I wash a shouting child's body.

A while later, after I am back in front of my computer, a knock comes at the door. Both of my children come in and ask to hold 2 rubber turtles they had gotten for me on a Father's Day past. I happily hand them over and when they have left, I stare back to the monitor.

I'm not really stuck. There's lots that I can write about. I have 2 children under 5 years of age, so a shortage of topics isn't what's happened. This isn't writer's block. Focus is what I'm lacking.

I remember a comment a reader made a few months back where she said how lucky my wife was to have a husband that was so in tune with his family. In actuality I'm the lucky one. Lucky enough to have a wife and family that support all the commonness that I radiate.

I have an average life that revolves from crisis to crisis. Some involve my family. Some not. All, though, are inextricably intertwined with the other.

Like most parents, at the end of the work day, it can be difficult for me to switch off the pressures of the job. The day's influences don't always wait at the office doorstep for my next day's return. Sometimes they tag along with me in the car ride home and up the walk. They can accompany me at the dinner table, while wrestling with my kids and even here in front of my keyboard.

What I'm trying to say is that just because I'm trying to write, it doesn't mean that I'm ready to. And perhaps a more painful confession is that on the other 6 nights, just because I'm with my kids doesn't mean that I'm set for a full night of quality parenting.

What I could use is some type of support group for fathers who are fixationally challenged. You know, those who want to leave the day's baggage at the door.

I recently received a note from one of my editors. In it she states that though she enjoys the content and humor of my columns, it would be okay if I tried some serious stuff now and again.

I hope this can suffice.

For the most part, I am just an average dad. I have stresses, and worries and wishes. Like you, I barely have enough time to read a column no less write one. And like you with the influences of bills, money, family and time, I don't believe that my life is facing a shortage of seriousness.

In fact, when it gets right down to it, levity shouldn't be underestimated.

May, 1996

Mike Grew Up

"BRRRRR... BRRRRR..." That's the sound you hear when you're waiting on the phone and no one on the other end has picked up.

It was 5:18 p.m. and I was in front of the home where this evening's babysitter resided. I was supposed to pick her up at 5:00, but several unanswered knocks on the door told me that the house was empty. A picture window in the living room was a framed stage where the curtain had opened to a vacant play.

No one was home.

I had the father's work number and called on my car phone.

"BRRRRR... BRRRRR..."

We have no family in the area, so lining up a trustworthy sitter is important.

"BRRRRR... BRRRRR..." Needless to say, with each unanswered ring, the anxiety level rose.

"Cruises Plus, this is Michael." Mike has always been one of those guys who is able to maintain a sunny disposition while facing the worst of disasters. That happens to be the one quality I detest in him.

I have known Mike for over 20 years. We went to school together. We played together. We grew apart and then had the good fortune to grow close again.

His daughter is 13. My kids are 2 and 4. I thought it would be a good match for sitter and sittee.

At the time though, I thought this might have been the chance where I would figuratively smack that perennial smile right off the front of his sunny disposition.

"Mike, old buddy," I gently whispered. "It's 20 after 5 and I was supposed to pick up Shanon at 5. I'm in front of your house and no one is home. Where the (@#*&%!) is she?"

75

"Ray," he answered with undiminished enthusiasm. "Shannie's here at the office. This was where you said you'd pick her up."

"Oh."

Because I was running late, I didn't have a chance to talk with Mike when I stopped for Shanon. I tapped the horn after I had pulled in and she ran right out. Mike and I exchanged brief waves as I backed out into the street.

The rest of the evening went pretty well. We showed Shanon where to find the emergency release forms and emergency numbers. She was then instructed on the proper protocol for diaper disposal and bedtime. We eventually were ready for our date right on time at 6:30 SFT, Standard Family Time. Exactly 60 minutes late.

It was an evening of mixing and mingling at a community event, and we didn't leave for home until the last dance was danced. Upon our return, we found all was well and, with the aid of a Pooh Bear or two, our little angels had settled quietly.

After Shanon and I had wrestled over the small bag of gold bullion that was to be her pay, I drove her home. The evening was late for even a 13-year-old, and because of this the drive was quiet.

When I had dropped her off, the living room curtain was still open and an inside light was on. I waited a few moments for a flickering porch light to signal that our sitter had entered safely. When nothing happened, I assumed Shanon must have gone back to the kitchen because I hadn't seen her cross over to the hall entrance.

I anxiously waited a few more seconds.

I was about to get out of the car when I saw Michael's head poke in from the hall. He said something to the back of the house and then stepped into the living room. He was dressed in his night wear and had paused in front of the window for a moment. He was still focused on the back of the house.

This time the stage held a silent film clip. A father waiting up for his daughter. The living room light had cast a shade on Michael I don't think I had seen before. I was surprised to find tears welling.

A moment later he turned to his audience of one, and with his all too characteristic smile, waved and disappeared down the hall, off stage.

I waved back to a blank window and fought back more tears. For a split second, his smile was a home movie of that young friend from my childhood. The boy I had grown up with. As I drove away on the back lit street, I was happy to have found the man he had become.

June, 1996

Family Vacations

"Everybody in the car? Okay, buckle up then. By my calculations, it should only take us 18 hours, 53 minutes and 17 seconds until we arrive at the Trees of Birch Bark Toilet Paper Campground. But that's only if we make two potty stops."

That's the way we always started our family vacations. We would all pile in the back of our Plymouth station wagon at 3 in the morning amid total darkness, only to emerge in an equally lightless evening. The time between was spent fighting with my siblings in the back seat or sweltering with our slobbering collie, Splash, in the very back. Dad always made certain the back window was rolled down enough so the dog and I got just the right mix of carbon monoxide.

We always returned, though, with wonderful stories of mishaps and vacations gone wrong. I think that's probably the best part of those trips, the calamities we keep next to our hearts.

Some things never change. Later this summer I hope to slog my kids into the car at some late night hour with the hopes they sleep through the drive. We won't pull off the highway until my children's bladders have stretched to three times their normal size.

This is the '90s though, and one can't stop evolution. The length of my parents Plymouth was equal to the ninth fairway at Pebble Beach. In fact from the dual headlights in the grill to the tail fins it was a chromium par four.

Today, our little import wagon could be tied to the Plymouth's roof rack. Our little wagon is also without a roll down rear window. My children will forever be deprived of the carbon monoxide euphoria that always took the edge off my childhood holidays.

For that matter, where we had free roam of the area behind the front bench seat, my cheerful little travelers have to be strapped into a car seat that only allows full radial mobility of their eyeballs.

The stories, however, will always warm their way into our memories.

The first vacation I can remember, my family traveled around the United States in the Plymouth with three kids, Splash, and an 18-foot travel trailer. I was still in diapers.

The tale tied to this trip involves a stop we made so the family could relieve themselves. Shortly, the car was loaded, and we were back on the road. My mother hadn't noticed that the car was unusually quiet until we were near the next town. It was then that it dawned on her we had left my 8-year-old brother back at the gas station.

My wife recalls a trip her family made to Lake of the Woods when she was young. They were traveling the highway in their Ford Falcon wagon. Her brother held a Porky Pig doll that belonged to my wife's sister. On occasion he dangled it out the window. When he tired of seeing his little sister's eyes bulge out of her head, he sang this harmless ditty.

"Porky Pig out the window for one week! Porky Pig out the window for two weeks! Porky Pig out the window forever!" And with that he set poor Porky free to fend for himself on the rough roadside of life.

Because my wife was predisposed to motion discomfort, most of her recollections focused on the brown bottom of a paper bag. That is one of the few memories my wife has of family trips.

As I said, soon I will wake my children before the sun has risen. I will belt them in while their thoughts are still dreaming. I'll fill the travel mug with coffee and quietly start the engine. Before pulling out of the drive, I'll take one more peek into the back seat. When their little eyes flutter, I'll know the time is right.

"Everybody in the car? By my calculations, it should only take us 17 hours, 25 minutes and 6 seconds until we arrive at Mosquito Mountain Campground. But that's only if we make two potty stops."

July, 1996

Southside

"Welcome!" Laura Adams shouted. "Welcome to the Southside Family Resource Center!"

The invitation stated it was the grand opening ceremony. I think it might have been a bit more.

I have spent some time over the past months doing a modest amount of volunteer work for Parent Education Network. Because of this, I was invited to join the grand opening ceremony of the Southside Family Resource Center.

Parent Education Network is a not-for-profit organization that provides a whole host of services to families of all income levels. These programs cover such areas from simple parent support groups all the way to in-home life skills management classes. Sometimes it's just having someone to talk to. Other times it's teaching how to keep a safe and sanitary home.

This grand opening ceremony was for another program that operates under P.E.N.'s umbrella. In truth, I can't remember the real name of the particular grant/program. It's some acronym that doesn't give justice to the good that is done. In design, the program is to work with a "community" to help make things better.

The Southside is an area that has more than its fair share of challenges. Hurdles that it has faced for a good part of its history. For the most part these problems are economic, social, and societal. Some might even venture to say moral.

You might think the task Parent Education Network took on in the Southside was to go in and clean up all the problems and make Southside new again. In reality, the goal was more ambitious: to work with community members of Southside and give them the support to reclaim the economic, social, societal and moral foundations that had been lost. Simply stated, it is to help community members rebuild their community.

Much has been done to take such steps and a fair distance has been traveled. The importance of this grand opening ceremony was not to acknowledge a completion, but to celebrate the flagship of all the efforts, the Southside Family Resource Center.

The center is a building acquired, refurbished, rewired, repainted, replumbed, re-insulated, and in short, rebuilt solely by the efforts of the community. Over 150 names of volunteers and contributors appear on the back of the program. Its design is to be a community focal point where parents, children and families can go to help and to be helped, to love and to be loved, to teach and to learn.

What I witnessed in its grand opening was not so much a ceremony. It was a celebration, a celebration of community.

Laura Adams, who chorused our welcome, lives in the Southside. She is a believer. Her task as she stood in front of the microphone was to welcome us, you and me. Her words told us that it was more than ceremony, even more than celebration. It was belief.

"Welcome!" she shouted. "Welcome... to the Southside Family Resource Center. Welcome... to our extended family. Welcome... to our dreams!"

July, 1996

Playdough

One of my favorite quotes says that a father's words are not heard by the world, but by posterity. I think one could also say that a father's actions are not necessarily heard by posterity ... but heard at day care.

It was a few weeks back that my children, wife and I were playing with playdough in the converted garage we now call our play room. My wife and I formed little rabbits and snails with spiraled shells. My 2-year-old son would then run them through the press, while my 4-year-old daughter cut out stars, Santas and reindeer. These were made from the cookie cutters we found in the holiday box.

The playdough was homemade: 2 cups flour, 1 cup salt, 2 cups water, a little cooking oil and cream of tartar, all topped off with some food coloring.

Green in general. FD&C yellow No. 5 and FD&C blue No.1 to be more exact.

My wife had mixed it up the day before, and we had just recently taken it out of the fridge.

Eventually, the animals, Santas and stars evolved back towards a more primitive playdough sculpture. Regardless of the dougher's age, education or upbringing, by the end of the doughing session, we always return to the point at which we all began. Indeed, there is nothing more refined in its simplistic beauty and versatility than a finely rolled playdough snake.

Delicately shaped between a tiny palm and the table top, the playdough snake is the ultimate survivor at any afternoon's doughing event. In fact, it wasn't until I had hand rolled a 6- or 7-inch radiant green beauty of my own, that I was jolted by a bolt of sheer paternal inspiration.

Fathers can be a proud sort.

I slowly turned away from my family with my green playdough snake. I raised my hands to my face and faked an enormous, Oscar winning sneeze. I turned back to my stunned family with my hands still covering my nose and chin.

"Honey," I said. "I think I need a tissue." Then, I pulled my hands away to reveal my 6 inch, lime green playdough reptile dangling from my right nostril.

My wife cringed, my children stood in awe, and for the next 30 minutes, I basked in the golden glow of fatherhood. I had reached the mountain's top and proudly held my head towards the heavens. If I had died that moment, I would have died a happy man.

The next week, my son went to preschool.

When my wife picked him up that afternoon, Jewell, the daycare director, gently pulled my wife aside and relayed a somewhat significant but harmless chain of events. It seems that, earlier in the day, the class was playing with playdough on the tables.

Innocent enough?

At one point, though, our young son became agitated and dismayed. He had placed a small amount of playdough up his nose in jest, and then became alarmed upon retrieval. The playdough had simply become lodged.

Thankfully, with God's blessing and two or three of Jewell's tissues, the demonic dough became unstuck and within a few minutes, my son regained full composure.

After hearing all this, my wife held a bemused look on her face.

"Well," my wife said. "I don't know where he would have learned to do that." Family image is important to my wife.

At this point my daughter reached up and grabbed my wife's sleeve. After several tugs and a few "MAMA's!" shouted, both Jewell's and my wife's attention were focused on her.

"Mama," my little angel beamed. "Daddy did. Daddy showed him how to put it up his nose. Remember?"

It's a comfort to me that my children view me as a source of knowledge and inspiration. And to think I am a model to be held in front of such tender minds is an achievement earned that I had never dreamed.

It makes me wonder sometimes. When all this is said and done and I look to tomorrow and to the parents my children will become, it is then I ask myself a simple question.

Exactly how long is posterity?

September, 1996

George's Father

The exhibit contained star thistle and fence posts, road signs and reflections, flowers and an older man. Delicate watercolors that shade views of rooms, space and life. Windows one might sense as an underlying theme.

Under each painting a little square held both title and dollar.

Hayfork - $900.

Jacob's Window - $1,200.

They hung on one wall mostly. I believe they faced east towards the new day. A current hummed through the room and pushed a steady stream of viewers tumbling past tables and chairs. The tables were like boulders supporting huge bowls of ice cream and toppings. The chairs were smaller rapids that sometimes held people. A nook against a counter provided an eddy where friends and admirers swirled about for a minute or two until they were swept up by the current and whisked downstream.

That's where I found George. In the little back water amid the gentler tide. Happily he was leaning back. One elbow anchored him to his Formica shore.

This was George's first art show since retiring. A show that, perhaps, was 70 years in the making.

I floated a little on the rim of the pool. I took a few turns on the outside and simply listened. Questions were asked of paintings and purpose. Answers were bold and muted. Advice was offered.

"Start right now. We're at the age where we have the confidence in ourselves to be comfortable with who we are."

In another moment I was swept away. I floated downstream past *Parade* and a bit beyond *Salt and Pepper.* I stopped when I came face to face with an old man. His hair was thinning and what was left, faded white. He stood bare-chested with the confidence that only a man of his age could have. His arms were extended out and his hands held a billowing yellow shirt. Its end was open and yawning, and the old man seemed to be peering inside.

Yellow Shirt —NFS

I looked over my shoulder and fixed my destination on the artist. Then, I began to paddle upstream.

When I reached the tranquil backwater, I extended a hand to George, and as he shook it I steadied myself on a neighboring stretch of Formica. We talked a little about his work and the hours that went into each painting. George spoke of theme and color. I admired the realism.

"Star thistle seems to be the favorite," George told me. "Everybody likes that one." A moment later he added with a Cheshire grin, "That one's mine." And he pointed at the man and the yellow shirt.

"That's my dad." George went on to tell me his father had passed away in 1985 at the age of 94. The portrait was painted from a picture taken when he was in his early 80's.

"It had to be," he told me. "You can't remember how they really looked so many years ago. I like that one most because I really captured him. Not so much how he looked, but how he was."

I looked across the room at George's father for a few moments, and when I turned back, I told George I saw a man who looked at the world like it was a yellow shirt. And though he knew it belonged to him, like the yellow shirt, he held it up in front of himself to look at it before he pulled it on.

George then quietly smiled and nodded his head. Then, out of either sincerity or politeness he added, "Yep. That's pretty much him."

I thanked George for his time and wished him congratulations on the turnout. A moment later I let go of my Formica beach and floated back towards the stream.

I often think of familial love flowing from parent to child. Though I love my father and admire the work and tears he has put into raising me and my siblings, my passions run to my children.

I think that it's all part of God's plan.

With George I know this is also true. To see him with his son or daughter or his grandsons, Daniel or Jake of *Jacob's Window,* you'd have no doubt. But I also admire the man who has learned from his father to hold his passions high for everyone to see.

September, 1996

Buying a Bike

I love to ride bicycles.

The simple joy of pumping pedals for locomotion is a therapy that takes physical fulfillment to a level of mental wellness I can't find in other activities. I believe if there is a heaven, it glides on two wheels, has coaster-brakes, whitewalls, and big, fat fenders.

I hope bicycling will be a passion passed on to my children. At present, I have some doubts, but I'm able to see glimmers of opportunity.

It was five months ago my wife and I set off to look for a big girl bike for my daughter. At 4 years of age, we thought she was ready to leave the security and stability of three wheels for the promise of independence and esteem that two proudly held. The plan was to load the kids in the back seat of the car and scour the day's garage sales.

After five hours and 54 gray hairs, we eventually returned to the morning's first garage sale. My wife got out to see if the little white Huffy was still available. I stayed in the car.

After three minutes of hardened negotiations, my wife returned to announce she had haggled the price down from the morning's asking price of $10 to a bargain basement $7.

A savings of 30 percent.

After we returned home and ate a quick lunch, my wife put my son down for a nap, and my daughter and I went to the store. A few things were needed to buff the lackluster of garage sale into the shining spirit of a big girl bike. Tires and tubes, training wheels, handgrips, streamers, and a white plastic basket with flowers were what was on the list.

Later that afternoon, my little cyclist sat upon her trusty steed. A helmet crowned her golden curls, whitened knuckles rolled over the curves of handle grips, and a happy smile spread across both our faces. Training wheels bolstered any fears either of us had.

That afternoon I held the back of the seat while my daughter pedaled down a neighboring cul-de-sac.

We were loving riding bicycles.

The next day we decided to have an adventure and go to the park to cruise the bike trails. I walked behind her for the first 10 minutes or so and then I thought the time was right for us to ride together. A favorite swimming hole was picked as the half-way destination. It was a place where we would rest, have some juice and cheese, and savor the day's accomplishments. My daughter had not faltered once.

Then it was time to ride back.

"No!" she screamed as the cooler was packed. "I hate riding bikes."

"No!" she screamed as we pushed the bicycles back onto the bike trail. "I'll fall!"

"No!" she screamed as I buckled her helmet.

"No!" she screamed as I put her on her refurbished white Huffy. "NOOOOOOOOOOOOOOOO!"

We rode our bikes all the way back to the truck, and though she didn't fall once, she screamed a tortured cry as if each turn of the pedal jolted her with electricity.

Other families pedaled past us with half smiles. By this time her screaming was nearly unintelligible. You could see the concern etched into their faces. I felt that, once passed, they would be talking of the abusive father who would torture such a young child. They might even call Child Services.

"He's riding a green Schwinn," they might say. "She'll be on a white Huffy with silver tassels and an orange Goofy horn."

I believe that was the longest quarter mile I have ever ridden on a bicycle.

As we loaded the bikes into the back of the truck, my daughter made it clear she did not savor my feelings toward cycling. She swore she would never ride a bike again, and carried on endlessly about the dangers involved for someone as young as she.

"Daddy," she told me. "I'm not riding a bike until I'm 10. It's too dangerous."

Her bicycle stayed in the garage for many weeks after that. For a long time she would have nothing to do with it and instead rode her undersized tricycle.

Recently, however, her interest has become renewed. Though we haven't made it back to the park, she is now able to gracefully glide the smooth pavement of the cul-de-sac.

I suppose there is hope that someday my daughter might have the love I have for pedaling the lanes of tree lined streets. She has even given her two-wheeled friend a name. "Rose Pedal" is what she calls it. Really.

I love riding bikes.

October, 1996

BEARS DON'T READ

The bears were supposed to read.

At least that was what my wife had heard when she had picked up our daughter from school. Another mother had announced, that fateful afternoon, that the Berenstain Bears were supposed to be at a local bookstore to read bedtime stories to the kids.

For those who may be bruinally challenged, the Berenstain Bears are fictional characters created by Jan and Stan Berenstain. They tell tales of Mama, Papa, Brother and Sister Bear's familial adventures in a happy hollow called Bear Country.

On that particular evening, Mama and Papa Bear were supposed to be at the bookstore to read to all of the children who braved the inky darkness of a sprinkling Friday evening.

I had arrived home from work at the usual time when, to my surprise, my normally docile and demure little angels from heaven were shouting at the top of their cherubic lungs that we were already late for a quickly approaching date with the previously described, scholastically endowed Ursidae Carnivora Berenstainus.

If we had a quick dinner, we could make it in time to what had then become, a forrestial habitat for both book and bear. Not to mention, the clerk who answered the phone told us to arrive ahead of time to ensure a venue close enough to be enjoyed without the aid of binoculars.

After I changed into more comfortable reading attire, the wife and I manically dressed the kids, threw them into the car, and dashed off to the nearby manuscript market. We arrived in time to grab a couple of seats in the third row of crossed legged critters with a full 23 minutes to spare before the appointed reading hour.

I think that was the first inkling where I sensed the doom that was to eventually settle on our gala. Twenty three minutes is a long time for our little angels to indulge themselves in any activity, let alone one whose sole focus was patience.

Within moments we could feel the faint tremors of a massive squiggle that could hold the sheer power to demolish four city blocks. Miraculously, order was maintained while the room became even fuller with the shouts and bounds of little Berenstain scholars. Fifty or 60 children had, if not quietly, efficiently packed themselves around the makeshift dais, while their parents, grandparents, brothers or sisters anxiously milled about the fray.

I settled next to Grandma Judy, a kindly woman who volunteers at the school my daughter attends. I know Grandma Judy to be the type of woman who has room in her heart for all the children in the world and a warm smile to share with every stranger she meets. My kids sat beside her grandchildren.

Seven o'clock found two chairs set with a microphone resting off to the side. At 7:05 a younger bookish woman dressed in black leggings, black skirt and a Century 21 gold colored blouse took the stage and picked up the microphone.

"Missy and Chrissy will now read a collection of Berenstain books while the Berenstain Bears themselves are now waiting to greet you waaaaayyy over at the other end of the room. You know, just past all those narrow rows of children's books." That may not be an exact quote.

The room became engulfed in spontaneous combustion as children jumped and clamored their way over the few unsuspecting tots who were actually expecting to hear a story read and the indiscernible shouts each parent screamed to themselves as a preschool riot began to unfold.

"WHAT IS THAT &*%$#@ LUNATIC THINKING!" we all screamed from our hearts if not our lips. "THESE KIDS HAVE

BEEN PACKED IN HERE FOR 23 &*%$#@ MINUTES WAIT-
ING FOR THE &*%$#@ BEARS TO READ, AND NOW YOU
TELL US THAT TWO FRESHLY POST PUBESCENT WOMEN
ARE GOING TO DO THE DRAMATIC INTERPRETATION,
WHILE THE &*%$#@ BEARS ARE WAAAAAYYY OVER
THERE! WHO'S GOT THE BOILING OIL?"

I quickly looked over to Grandma Judy to see how this battle
scarred veteran would negotiate the melee that was sure to follow.
Smoke poured out of Judy's ears and laser death rays shot from her
eyes at the black and gold, bibliophilic blonde, and burned her
into an incendiary black hole at the back of the bookstore.

For the next 20 or 30 minutes, my wife and I chased our kids
around the store while we intermittently tried to snap pictures of
them next to the Berenstain Bears in their natural habitat. We
caught snippets of Missy or Chrissy pleading with the children to
"Please return the books and the microphone," so they could continue the reading.

I thought about the evening the whole way back to the house, trying to understand what hidden message there could have been in
the chaos experienced that night. What was I to glean from what
happened?

It wasn't until much later I discovered the truths to be learned.
My head was on the pillow, and I leaned over to turn off the light.
There, in the darkened silence of my room, it finally came to me.

Bears were never meant to read.

February, 1997

LUNCH

There is nothing more glorious than to lunch with a good friend over a cold glass of milk, and peanut butter and jelly, while the candlelight's shadows dance about the room.

I have the good fortune to eat lunch out quite often. My job requires I take clients, or prospective clients, out for the mid-day meal. The idea is to set aside some time to talk over business proposals, strategies and perhaps, blueberry cheesecake. I give them food. They give me 20 to 30 minutes in which I have the chance to share my ideas.

More if I eat fast.

The company I work for patronizes nearly a dozen eateries throughout town where the check is simply initialed and then sent on to the bookkeeper. And in case those diners don't satisfy a client's more particular pangs, there is an expense account with little limitations as to the caliber of restaurant in which to satiate said clients' culinary desires.

I wouldn't be honest if I said that I didn't eat well at lunch. I would be fibbing if I were to say I have actually been losing weight. I would be lying if I told you eating out never got old.

While I'm not complaining, I think it's fair to say that under these circumstances, lunch can sometimes be a little like Christmas. If you had Christmas every day, it wouldn't be Christmas anymore.

The other day, though, I had the good fortune to break away from the wholly, white collared tradition of edible bribery. My wife was running behind and was unable to pick up our daughter from school. I was to meet my daughter at 11:25. After that, my wife was to arrive home by 12:30.

On the way back from kindergarten, my daughter read to me from a book she had written earlier that day and shared a few pictures she had drawn. When we had arrived home, we quickly went into the house, and while I started to make a sandwich for my daughter, she went in to herd up a loose band of Barbies that had meandered across the great Hi-Low plains that we call our play-room carpet.

It was the first sunny day in a week's worth of wicked weather, and I thought it would be a nice treat to sit out back at the picnic table and enjoy the warmth of the outdoors. As I opened the door though, I was reminded our septic system had been backed up for the past day or so, and in our backyard lay an old and decayed leach line, freshly exposed.

Time for plan B.

I went back into the playroom and pushed the Fisher Price table into the rays of sunshine that poured through the south window.

"Honey?" I asked. "How about we do something special and eat here in the playroom? Right at the table in the warm sunshine?"

For a moment, my daughter lifted her head from the impas-sioned gaze of a dozen love struck Barbies.

"No," she said. "That's okay." And she went about her Barbie business. A few moments later though, without lifting her head she spoke again.

"Maybe," she hesitated. "Maybe we could light some candles and eat in the dining room." She then looked up at me and smiled. "That would be special."

My daughter and I enjoyed a quiet sandwich together that af-ternoon. A feast that would become a milestone in my noon time meals. Indeed, there is nothing more glorious than to lunch with a good friend over a cold glass of milk, and peanut butter and jelly, while the candlelight's shadows dance about the room.

February, 1997

A Delicate Matter

When I sit down to write a column, sometimes I get stuck. My mind will draw a blank as it scours the barren wasteland of my creative resources. Then, as if I'm hit in the head with a box of rocks, a flash sent from heaven will jolt me with 50 bazillion volts of inspiration.

Tonight started off as one of those nights. I was chewing my nails as the deadline loomed, and prayed for the smallest of thoughts to pop into the artistic horizon.

Then the telephone rang.

"Jeff's on the phone." My wife peeked in from behind the door. "He said he has something delicate to talk to you about."

My eyebrows peaked with curiosity.

Jeff is a friend who has a son and daughter who are roughly the same distance apart in age as my children. Jeff's boy just turned 3 and his daughter is less than 1. My daughter is now 5, while my son recently celebrated his 3rd birthday. We sometimes get together for a barbecue or a romp in the park. On occasion, Jeff and I have taken a break from work to treat our sons to lunch.

Just us boys.

Now though he had something delicate he wanted to talk about.

I last saw Jeff not even a week ago. I pulled into a gas station to fill up. Once I had the nozzle in the tank with the gas flowing, I noticed that Jeff and his son were filling up the family mini van on the other side of the island. The back hatch was open and Jeff's happy little guy was bouncing and hopping from the front seats all the way to the rear opening and back again.

I waved.

When we talked, we spoke of weekend plans and upcoming family events. Shortly though our conversation turned to a rather common topic for happy dads like us; fathers who are in our mid to late 30s, in the passionate throws of parenthood and struggling each and every month to feed our family, make the mortgage payment and have a little left over for beer and pork rinds.

That topic would be vasectomies.

There was no doubt Jeff was going to have the procedure done. At this point he just needed to settle on the doctor and wrestle up the confidence.

"My insurance covers Johnson but you have to go in for some counseling sessions first." Jeff tends to normally be very animated when he talks, but I had to notice that he was pacing from one foot to the other in a rather exaggerated tempo.

"Lagendorf is good too, though," he added and nodded his head as if to agree with himself.

I, too, have considered making the cut in recent months. My wife and I are very happy with our family, and we have grown somewhat content as we are now able to enjoy a minimum of six solid, uninterrupted hours of sleep each night. A vasectomy appeared to be a logical step.

I have to be honest here though. As our talks continued, I was reminded of the sensation I felt back in sixth grade when I ran my bicycle into the backyard gate. I too, began to pace.

A few minutes later, my gas nozzle shut off and our conversation stumbled upon a somewhat awkward pause.

"I wonder... ," I said to myself more than anybody. "If it would cost less if we went in together? Like a bulk rate?"

And now, almost one week later, Jeff was waiting for me on the phone with something delicate he wanted to talk to me about.

Boy, talk about your inspiration!

"Hey Jeff," I said after I had picked up the phone.

"Hi," he responded in a staccato frenzy. "I found out Dr. Johnson is retired and Lagendorf is the only other one my insurance will cover." I could tell Jeff was trying to be subtle. "I just thought that you might want to check with your insurance to see if he'd be covered, and maybe we could ... you know, go in together."

I could tell Jeff was pacing.

"Really?" I said. And without a second to breathe, Jeff jumped right back in.

"He's a good doctor. Small hands too. And you know, afterwards, we might go and celebrate with some Rocky Mountain Oysters."

"Well," I was trying to take notes here. You know. Just in case. "How soon?"

"Oh, anytime. You know, in the next 10 years."

"Is Lagendorf the one who does the counseling?"

"No. That's Johnson. But he's retired now. We wouldn't have to do the counseling. I mean, do I have to prove that I have the balls to go through with it, or would they just have to count and take measurements?"

Jeff wasn't just pacing, I think he might have been wearing a hole in the hardwood.

I shouldn't lead you to believe I remained calm and stoic here. Though I have considered altering the physical makeup of my nether region on more than one occasion, I didn't think it was time to make the decision yet.

I told Jeff I would look in our insurance guide to see if Lagendorf was approved and would call him back in the next day or two. I then glanced to my watch and noticed that I was now six and a half minutes closer to my impending deadline.

Jeff?" I asked rather casually.

"Yeah?

"Would it be okay if I used your real name in my column?"

April, 1997

Graduation Overnight

There are times that come where ceremony is required to mark a passage from one stage in life to another. A time where friends and companions are gathered near to celebrate, in communion, a step to be taken that will leave a part behind and wholly embrace what lies ahead. A graduation, if you will, to acknowledge the accomplishments made in anticipation of the next shining horizon.

It is rare enough when I am privileged to be a member of such an illustrious brotherhood, but rarer still where I am tapped to be a witness of such a fellowship for my children.

I find it remarkable that my daughter is on the eve of finishing her kindergarten curriculum and ready to move on to the regimen and structure of grade school. I find it remarkable that her classmates unflinchingly stand at her side as, they too, look towards the promise of next year. I say remarkable because it was but a few months ago these same students were gently ushered in with eyes wide and hands held tight only to be left behind with anxious pacings and trembling lower lips.

Remarkable how our children have made such enormous strides in so little time.

On a quiet summer's eve, my daughter, and her classmates celebrated their graduation with just such a ceremony. A slumber party for the graduating class of 2009 held in the hallowed halls where these young minds found an irrepressible sense of independence, discovered love in friendship, and learned the heady sense of pride nurtured in the acquisition of knowledge.

Room 18.

Think of it as a post-toddler "Friday Night Live" with Mickey Mouse instead of Madonna, and Raffi instead of rap.

I was a chaperone.

For the entire week before, almost nothing else was talked about at our dinner table. It was a night to be filled with videos and cookies, games and treats.

"We'll even stay up until midnight!" my daughter proudly boasted.

As the day approached anticipation grew and grew. We ticked off the lists of items required:

Sleeping bag - √ Toothbrush - √ Pajamas - √ Bunny - √

On the evening of, backpacks, hers and mine, were packed. We loaded them into the car and headed out serenaded not by the formal pacing of "Pomp and Circumstance," but by the swaggering, "I've Been Working on the Railroad."

We were greeted by Mrs. Starkey at the door. Our dish of oatmeal-butterscotch cookies was placed next to a pile of goodies heaped with watermelon slices, broccoli, baby carrots, Gummy Bears and bubble gum.

Grandma Judy, the ever-present aid in my daughter's class, gently guided us to my daughter's cubby, so we could place our packs out of the way. The sleeping bags and pads were tossed onto a growing mountain in the corner of the room, and once freed of them, we settled ourselves on the floor.

After we had been seated, we made beautiful music.

A box was placed in the center of our circle and everyone found an instrument to play. I had bells while my daughter alternated between maracas and wood sticks. All the while Mrs. Starkey conducted as music played in the background.

"Wood sticks and bells!" she would shout as we roared our instruments into a furious crescendo.

"Sandpaper blocks and triangles ..." she whispered. Pianissimo.

The rest of the night was filled with bubbles and egg races, ribbon dancing and storybooks.

And we sang songs as a flashlight softly glowed through tissue paper flames. And when a camera's flash lightninged across our night sky, I counted the miles until we heard Grandma Judy's thunder as her palms rumbled along a filing cabinet's side.

"Flash!"

" One, two, three, four, five ..."

"brrroooOOOMMMM!"

And when the paper fires had died down, we readied ourselves for bed.

As we lay in our little bags on the floor of Room 18, I hoped my daughter's sleep would be filled with dreams of the joys she had found in the past year and the anticipations of those that are to follow.

As for me, I found the night held not just a graduation of children, but something more. Yes, it was a ceremony of passage, but more importantly, I think it was a celebration of childhood. And as I listened to the tiny voices whispering in a darkened room, I also discovered it was a childhood I was not just asked to witness but one I was invited to share.

June, 1997

Paper or Plastic

Boy! Talk about your generation gaps.

Last weekend my father came to visit. Shortly after he arrived, I needed to pick up a few things from the store, so I asked Dad if he wanted to go along. When all of the items were selected, we stood at the checkout counter waiting for everything to be rung up.

A father and son, side by side. The son, a father in his own right, held his head high in an effort to show how he could make his way in a sometimes cruel and heartless world. The elder watched to behold and weigh what type of man he had raised to burden the responsibilities of parenthood.

"Paper or plastic?" The bagger addressed my father.

"Paper." I said without hesitation. I looked to my father and added, "Good thing I answered. You might have gotten the wrong one."

"You're right," he responded. "I would have gotten plastic. With those I can carry four bags. With paper I can only carry two."

It was time for me to show my control of the elements. Time to prove myself.

"But plastic is bad for the environment," I explained. "Think of all the landfills."

"No," he said. "You take them to the recycling centers. That way you don't cut down trees."

I gave this a little thought, but to be honest, I couldn't get away from his triumph of being able to carry four bags. He couldn't possibly carry four bags. With all the weight the plastic would stretch around his joints and practically pinch his fingers off. But I couldn't bring that up and threaten his masculinity. Not at his age.

"Paper is so much easier to store," I countered. "You just fold them flat." I had him on the ropes now. It wasn't checkers in the rec room anymore.

"You're kidding? I can fit a hundred of them into one bag."

"Aha!" I exclaimed. He was in the palm of my hand now. "If you stick a hundred of them in, when you pull one out, you get the other 99 with it." He was at my mercy.

"No you won't," he said with a smug smile.

I was dumbfounded. How could he have said that. Facts are facts. He had to acknowledge that. I just had to lay it all out, and surely he would see the light.

"Yes you will!"

"Fine."

If there is a lesson to be learned in life, it is that you can't just say "Fine" in the throws of an argument and expect everyone involved to be fine with it. I couldn't let him off that easy. It was time to pull out the big guns. No let up for the old man now. He threw the gauntlet, and now it was time to mop him up.

I had hoped it wasn't going to come to this.

"Okay," I said in a voice cloaked with victory. "Let's see you stand up a plastic bag in the back yard, so you can dump dog poop into it."

His brow furrowed, and his lips tightened. He looked away. What I saw was the actions of a man badly beaten, a man struggling to save not just face and composure, but his very essence.

A moment later when he looked back, he said, "You're right on that one. It would have to be paper."

It wasn't until we were driving home it hit me. We weren't talking about the difference of bags as much as we were the difference in generations.

Mine is the boomer generation. I grew up watching the lunar landings on TV. My father's generation was the one whose efforts not only put men on the moon, but created the technology that allowed me and a bezillion other boomers to watch in the air conditioned comfort of our homes.

He was the participant, I was just an observer.

Maybe this illustrates it was my father and his colleagues whose forward thinking took us out of the Depression and whose work made things as best as things could possibly be. Maybe my friends and I were just along for the ride.

Maybe, and maybe not.

Perhaps we're just more sentimental. Could it be that we do look forward to what tomorrow will bring, but aren't ready to throw out the standbys of today?

Truth be told, maybe we just like to be out on a crisp fall morning, enjoying the fresh air with tools in hand, knowing that a sturdy and time tested paper bag is faithfully waiting on the lawn.

July, 1997

A Poem Found

A story told.

Just words shared with another. When written down it can be held and lifted high above for anyone to see. And in doing so, it may no longer be a simple story told but something much more.

My fondest memories
my family,
Born to Homer and Helen,
my sister,
Beverly Jean,
and home.

A father answers questions for his child. A story is told and notes are made. Memories written on paper or perhaps colored somewhere deeper. An indelible mark on a more personal parchment.

Born in Long Beach,
moved to Cleveland,
and back again.

How else to know where we came from? How else to learn about ourselves, our histories? No where could we find a more valuable lesson.

Moved in with Aunt Alida
Awfully poor
Got a rental
Credit for
a can of beans.

Here we discover the blocks that were used to build our lives. This is how we learn of the people who brought life to us. Hear the threads that had been woven for our fabric. Each color brought a hue of its own and combined to make a wonderfully woven quilt.

Dad
sold Kirbies
helped build aircraft
sold reclaimed oil.
The business wasn't a success
but it kept us fed.

Too often though, when tales are told, they are only held briefly. The preoccupations, and pressures of the day, fight for attention and steal away the details and intimacies. What was held so dearly by one, might indeed be lost. It wouldn't have taken long to write it down. A memory preserved in moments.

But there's not enough time.

Shep followed me home
Sort of a sheltie type
must have had her till I was 15
then she died.

What about that English class? The one from seventh, eighth grade, or maybe freshman year? What was that assignment? Interview a parent? Grandparent? Fill a page or two with notes that cover a lifetime. Flesh it out to meet the required pages, and do a bit of polish on structure and transitions.

And then what?

Mom let me drive down to irrigate
I forgot
The break?
The clutch?
Road turned and I went straight.

And then what?
Listen.
In a gentle voice, whether told over a kitchen table or stretched across miles, a painting will be found. Brushed in words and shaded with love. A beauty held not in hand but by heart.

Discipline?
I certainly wasn't an angel
I didn't get caught.
Dad just spanked.
Mom used the strap.

It will come matted in some muted shade and maybe bordered in some gaudy gilded frame. But look closer. See how it is caressed. Feel the warmth in its body. Touch the lyrical meter with which it is told.

Met her at the pig barn,
on the wrong bus.
I was the tour guide.
Asked her out later
at the library.

A tale unheard makes no listener want. A story lost makes the owner no poorer. A memory saved, however, is a fortune of immeasurable wealth.

Wedding Day
Uncle Pete got bit by the dog
Aunts and Grandma broke the sofa leg...
they're all heavy
Let's see married in '53
Was I twenty-five?

Listen. Can you hear the song that is sung? It is yours and told just for you. It can only take a moment to take a memory lost and turn it into a poem found.

June, 1997

*P*arent *E*ducation *N*etwork

It all begins with family . . . .

Who we are, what we care about, what we expect from ourselves and those around us . . . our core beliefs are formed at home among the people who first welcome us into the world. The family's hold upon our hearts and minds is mysterious, irresistible; its power to shape the course of our lives is beyond measure.

Parent Education Network, a not-for-profit organization, recognizes and respects the meaning of family. Since 1980, we have been helping families, offering parent education, counseling, child development programs, child care, community development, and training for professionals, para-professionals, and community residents. Our professional and volunteer staff are dedicated to helping create safe, secure homes from which parents and children can draw vitality and hope.

We count on the generous contributions of caring individuals to continue serving children and families. Your tax deductible gift will provide hope to a child in need. Know that together we can build a foundation of love and trust that parents and children will build upon for a lifetime. Thank you in advance for caring.

Name
_____

(   )
_____
phone (please include area code)

Address
_____

City
_____

State _____ Zip _____

*P*lease make your check payable to:
Parent Education Network
2592 Notre Dame Blvd., Suite B
Chico, CA 95928